THE FREE PEOPLE OF COLOR OF NEW ORLEANS

An Introduction

Mary Gehman

Photos by Lloyd Dennis

D'Ville Press LLC

Published by D'Ville Press LLC
Copyright Mary Gehman

Seventh edition 2017

Printed in the U.S.A. by
Emprint/Moran Printing, Inc.
Baton Rouge, LA

ISBN 978-0-9994589-0-7

Library of Congress 94-075007

D'Ville Press LLC
618 Mississippi Street
Donaldsonville, LA 70346
(225) 473-9319

Acknowledgements

This book is dedicated to the memory of two New Orleans researchers and writers whose work has formed a foundation for the current study of free people of color. Marcus Christian (1900-1976) headed the New Orleans Black Writers Project of the Works Progress Administration in the 1930s and left a book length unpublished manuscript "The Negro in Louisiana". Ulysses S. Ricard, Jr. (1950-1993) was a senior archivist at the Amistad Research Center and an expert on the Creoles; he personally encouraged the author in the writing of this book.

Acknowledgement of time, inspiration, advice and information are due the many friends, scholars and archivists who made this book possible. They include the staffs of the Louisiana Division of the Howard-Tilton Library at Tulane University, the Louisiana Historical Center of the Louisiana State Museum, the Louisiana Section of the New Orleans Public Library, Special Collections at the Library of the University of New Orleans, Xavier University Archives, the Amistad Research Center, and The Historic New Orleans Collection.

Special thanks to Beatrice Ausley, Mary M. White, Greg Osborne, Joan Caldwell, Richard Campbell, Lester Sullivan, Jane Moloney, Brian Howell, Sr., Sybil Kein, Katherine and Caroline Senter, Albertine Norwood, Frank McGuire, Charles Gandolfo and Orleans Colour Separation.

TABLE OF CONTENTS

A.P. Tureaud (1899-1972) of Creole heritage, attorney who was center of the civil rights movement in New Orleans and mentor for current black leaders. Photo courtesy of Amistad Research Center, N.O. where his papers are archived.

Introduction

There is no State in the Union, hardly any spot of like size on the globe where the man of color has lived so intensely, made so much progress, been of such historical importance [as in Louisiana] and yet about whom so comparatively little is known.

-Alice Dunbar Nelson 1916

New Orleans is referred to today by some travel writers as the most africanized city in the U. S. In its famous jazz music resound the rhythms of slave dances in Congo Square; in its tasty cuisine are the ingredients and flavors adapted by generations of African cooks; in its Caribbean-colonial style architecture are the touches of color, iron work, woodworking and brick fashioned by African artisans; and in the faces of its people are features and skin tones that reflect centuries of inter-racial mixing of African, Indian, Latin and European. The spirit of family, neighborhood and celebration that is the trademark of this unique city has deep psychological roots in the descendants of people who a century and a half ago lived in a three-tier system in Louisiana: white – free person of color – and slave.

The history of the whites and the slaves is fairly well known. What has remained in a fictional shadow is the middle group, *les gens de couleur libre* as the French named them, the free people of color, who after the Civil War were called Creoles of color, shortened today to simply Creoles. Numbering in the thousands in New Orleans of the early 1800s, the free people of

Introduction

Unique pavilion in Duncan Plaza near New Orleans City Hall is styled after the African House of Melrose Plantation (pages 40-41)

color had their own identity in a caste that was neither black nor white, neither slave nor entirely free. French speaking Catholics, well educated and middle class for the most part, they were respected members of New Orleans society who attended the French opera and theater, debated the latest politics in their own newspapers, and worshipped in the St. Louis Cathedral.

They include merchants Etienne Cordeviolle, Francois LaCroix and Dominique Mercier, real estate developers Drausin Barthelemy Macarty and Noel Carriere, literary figures like writer Armand Lanusse and dramatist Victor Sejour, musicians and composers Edmund Dédé and Basile Bares, actress Adah Isaacs Menken, stone sculptors Eugene and Daniel Warburg, inventor Norbert Rillieux, historian Rodolphe Desdunes, planters Aristide Mary, Louis Roquiny and Antoine Dubuclet, architect Louis Nelson Fouché, builders Joseph and Louis Dolliole, and philanthropist Thomy Lafon.

Many free men of color distinguished themselves as soldiers in the Battle of New Orleans, some owned slaves and joined the Confederacy in the Civil War. The free women of color were nurses, hair dressers and dressmakers to the upper class French ladies; at the same time many of these ladies' French husbands, sons and brothers had a shadow family among the young free women of color, set them up in small houses and fathered children with them, giving their natural offspring their same French surnames and passing on to them property and wealth.

New Orleans had by far the largest community of free people of color in the United States. Though many lived in outlying parishes throughout Louisiana, New Orleans was their center where they developed their own influential leaders who helped shape the social, economic, and legal history of the city as well as the state of Louisiana. In every regime, every change of government, the free people of color exerted their influence. During Reconstruction they are widely credited with having shaped national policies in Washington, D.C. on civil rights and suffrage for blacks. The influence and effects of these early statesmen are still felt today in local social and political circles that reach far outside New Orleans.

How did such a large number of slaves become free decades before the Civil War, and how did they acquire businesses and estates? What made all this possible in Louisiana and New Orleans but not in other parts of the South? This book is an attempt to answer those questions and to introduce readers to the lives and contributions of the free people of color rarely known and acknowledged. As an introduction, it is a chronological overview of their history with brief explanations of various terms and periods. It is by no means a conclusive history, since new information and understanding of this group of people is constantly emerging through contemporary academic research. The end notes and bibliography provided at the back of the book are intended for readers to continue their own study of these African-Americans for a more complete account of black history in the United States.

Straight University above, chartered in 1869 to educate blacks, merged with New Orleans University in 1935 to form Dillard University. Photo (1893) courtesy of Amistad Research Center.

Founding of New Orleans,
the Early Years 1718 - 1730

1699	Founding of Louisiana as a French colony
1702	Mobile established as capital of the colony
1718	Founding of city of New Orleans
1717-31	Company of the Indies aka Company of the West contracted by John Law to populate Louisiana
1719	First slave cargo brought to Louisiana: their work saves a struggling French community. 2083 slaves imported 1719-1723
1718-24	A few free blacks enter Louisiana via France or West Indies. Population of N.O. 1721: 248 whites, 172 slaves, 50 other (free blacks, Indians).
1722	Capital of Louisiana moves from Mobile to N.O.
1722	First record of free blacks in New Orleans
1723	Slaves ally with Natchez Indians against French
1724	Code Noir (Black Code) adopted: establishes rights of slaves and free blacks
1724	First record of free black suit in court

1725	First free black marriages in church
1729-30	Massacre at Port Rosalie: Natchez Indians and black slaves attack French at Natchez. French win
1730	Company of the Indies bankrupt, Louisiana reverts to France
1731	Slave revolt foiled in New Orleans

Founding of New Orleans, the Early Years 1718 - 1730

The first two decades of the city of New Orleans after its founding in 1718 were tumultuous and chaotic. Historians generally agree that several hundred African slaves owned by the Company of the West, that held the concession for populating and developing Louisiana, were crucial in pulling the remote French outpost through those dark years.

The vast Louisiana Territory had been claimed as a colony for the King of France nearly twenty years (1699) before the Scottish exile John Law convinced King Louis XIV to give his Company of the West (later called Company of the Indies) a 25-year charter to operate the colony. Jean Baptiste Lemoyne, Sieur de Bienville, a French Canadian, was named by Law to be director general of the colony. Within a year, Bienville set his sights on establishing a town on the lower part of the great Mississippi River that flowed the length of the Territory.

The high ground where the river made a large crescent-shaped curve about a hundred miles from its mouth into the Gulf of Mexico was chosen by Bienville as a suitable place to clear land and found the settlement *Nouvelle Orléans*, named in honor of the Duke of Orléans, a strong supporter of John Law. The site was already a well established trading post for various indigenous peoples (Indian tribes) in the area, such as the Choctaws, Colapissa, Houmas and Tunicas, and Bienville doubtless envisioned a thriving French port city.

It took Bienville and some fifty men he had collected

Colorful Mardi Gras Indians, who make new costumes every year, are a tradition in New Orleans and a tribute to alliances between runaway slaves and indigenous tribes in the 1700s.

several years to make the swampy environs into a habitable settlement. The project was greatly aided by several hundred Africans brought in 1719 on cargo ships from West Africa to Mobile, the Louisiana capital city along the Gulf, and routed to New Orleans. French and English colonies in the Caribbean had already established the institution of African slavery as a source for efficient laborers; some early slaves in Louisiana were imported from those colonies, but the majority came after 1716 (2,083 slaves from 1719-1723) on trading ships directly

By 1722 New Orleans had begun to take shape. Streets were laid out, the capital of Louisiana was moved there, and ships began arriving at the riverfront. Slaves imported to Louisiana were sought for their skills in cultivating rice, tobacco and indigo; these soon became staples shipped through the New Orleans port. [2]

The French subsisted under trying conditions in those early years, and their slaves suffered with them the lack of food, clothes and shelter. There was a scarcity of women, African or French, and single men of both races spent long periods of time with Indian tribes where they were fed and clothed. There they also found Indian women whom they frequently brought back to New Orleans to keep house for them and bear their children.

First Free Blacks Appear

From the very beginning of New Orleans there were some free blacks who came either from the Caribbean or via France. A few are believed to have come as servants with French families who settled in the city in the late 1720s; others found their way along the trade routes from the West Indian colonies of St. Domingue and Cuba. In 1722 the first record of a free man of color, Laroze, appears in New Orleans in a case of the colonial court. Laroze was tried and found guilty of stealing for which he was flogged and sentenced to six years in prison. After serving his sentence he was not re-enslaved, indicating that once a free person, his freedom could not be taken away.

Two years later the first record of a free man of color entering a suit against a white person appears; Raphael Bernard sued Paulin Cadot for money which Cadot owed him but

11

refused to repay. Bernard won the case, but whether Cadot ever paid up is not recorded. A year later, in 1725 there is the record of the marriage of Jean B. Raphael and Marie Gaspar in the parish church in New Orleans. Both Raphael and Gaspar were free persons of color. That same year the slave Louis Congo was freed by the King's orders to become the executioner for the Territory. It was a job which no white man wanted because the executioner's life was frequently threatened. In the 1726 census a year later, the free man of color Jean Congo is listed as the keeper of the High Road along Bayou St. John which was a waterway leading into New Orleans. He and his wife had a house along the bayou; their job reportedly involved collecting tolls from boats that passed into the city. [3]

The Black Code

The presence of these people of color in the earliest records of the city shows that not only were they free but they held professional positions, had access to the justice of the colonial court and owned property, qualities that would prove essential to their descendants in the subsequent hundred years. These rights were spelled out in the *code noir* or Black Code introduced in 1724 that prescribed how masters should treat their slaves, under what conditions freedom should be granted, and the rights and obligations of slaves once freed. Contrary to British law regarding slavery, the French code which had long been in effect in the West Indies, granted to Louisiana slaves the right to a religious (Catholic) education, redress in the colonial court for mistreatment by a master, and opportunities to be hired out by a master or to hire oneself out for wages. Slave marriages were recognized by the church, slave children were

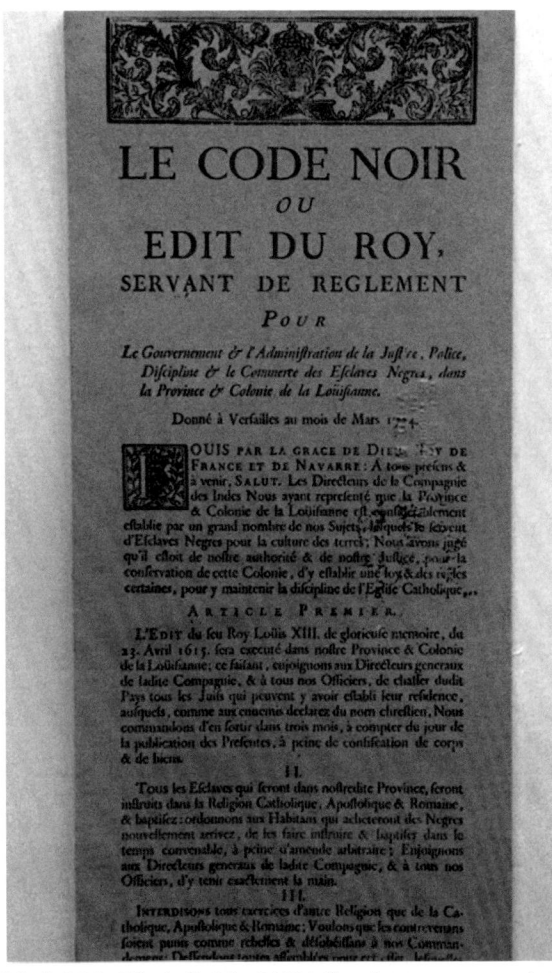

Copy of Code Noir (Black Code) of 1724 dictating treatment and rights of slaves and free people of color in Louisiana. Photo courtesy of Amistad Research Center.

baptized in the church, and slave families were not to be separated through sale. [4]

Once free, according to the Black Code, persons of color were granted the rights of full citizenship except for three crucial exceptions; they could not vote, hold public office or marry a white person. Because all non-whites had to carry proof of either ownership by a master or proof of being freed, free people of color were expected to carry passes identifying their status. They were also not allowed to own or operate establishments where alcohol was sold. Through the years there were additional rules added, sometimes formally, other times informally, to the Black Code, depending on the political temper of the time. There were periods when free blacks had to observe the slave curfew bell of 9:00 p.m., when they could not mask for balls and could not place wagers or bets of any form, when they had to gain permission to travel outside the city, or when they were prohibited from gathering in public.

The things they were permitted to do were constant and even more significant, for they could conduct all sorts of business, invest and lend out money, purchase and own slaves, attend French social institutions such as church, the theater and the opera. They could live and build houses anywhere they chose, open schools to educate their children and conduct their own dances, balls and social gatherings.

The Natchez Massacre

A very important event, the Natchez Massacre or Natchez War, closed out the era of the Company of the Indies in

1730. Again, the role of Africans was crucial in the outcome. John Law's bank was in serious trouble by 1723, and Law himself fled Louisiana with his creditors in hot pursuit. The Company was reorganized by the French government, and in 1727 Etienne de Perier took Bienville's place as commandant of Louisiana. Unlike his predecessor, Perier refused to recognize the Indian tribes' rights to their lands. The large Natchez nation to the north refused to surrender its fertile crop lands in the area of what is today Natchez, Mississippi.

Using the help and connections of some African slaves that had escaped to live with the Natchez tribe, the Indians attacked the French community of about 500 people at Fort Rosalie on the bluffs of the Mississippi River in the winter of 1729. Many French men were killed and their wives and children captured and tortured. Word of the conflict eventually reached Perier, who acted with swift retaliation. A detachment of over 700 fighters, many of them free blacks and slaves, was sent to kill as many Natchez as possible and rescue the captured French. As a reward for bravery, slaves were offered their freedom.

In that vicious confrontation of early 1730 a significant number of Natchez were killed. Even after the Natchez had surrendered and returned the surviving French captives, Perier's troops continued to decimate the Indian tribe so that by 1731 there were only a few Natchez alive. [5]

Slave Revolt Foiled

In the aftermath of Fort Rosalie, a slave revolt was planned in New Orleans, masterminded by some of the Africans who had escaped from the Natchez confrontation. Having lived in relative freedom with the Indians and having close ties with them, these returning slaves had learned several important things. They knew that the French in the various scattered settlements were not in a good position to defend themselves against attacks from within, they saw how far outnumbered whites were by blacks and Indians, how heavily whites depended on slave labor and how lost they would be without it, and they also had seen how the Indians repeatedly carried out successful raids against the whites. By the summer of 1731 carefully laid plans were in place for the slaves involved to slay all whites in their path north to south through Louisiana and to take over the government.

How close this plan came to realization is not certain, but had it succeeded, hundreds of lives would have been lost and the history of Louisiana drastically affected. A slave woman reportedly betrayed the conspiracy by bragging to a French soldier who had abused her, that he would not be alive to treat her that way much longer. Her comments led to an investigation of New Orleans slaves and the uncovering of the plot. Eight slave men marked as leaders of the revolt were killed in the manner of the day, breaking them on the wheel in the Place D'Armes in New Orleans, and the woman was hanged for her slip of the tongue. The heads of these conspirators were displayed on poles at various points along the Mississippi River to serve as a warning to any other slaves considering similar action against the French.

The French Period 1731-1762

1731	Company of the Indies bankrupt, colony reverts to France
1733	Earliest record of slave freed in Louisiana
1735-36	Blacks fight with French in Chickasaw War
1739	Blacks fight in second attack on Chickasaws
1740s	African market established by slaves in Place des Negres (today Congo Square)
1740	Slave trade direct from Africa almost closed
1751	Police code issued re behavior of blacks
1754-63	Seven Years' War in Europe: trade with France halted
1760	King's slaves in Louisiana sold, end of municipal slave force
1762	Louisiana transferred from French to Spanish rule

The French Period 1731-1762

The first time in colonial Louisiana that Africans received formal recognition for service was after the Natchez war of 1730. Dozens of African slave men who had fought valiantly with the French were awarded their freedom, and those black troops already free were given special recognition for military service to the French crown. Not all Africans, however, took advantage of this opportunity to prove themselves fighters, and gain their freedom; a contingent of slaves continued to ally themselves with the Indians, running away to live with various tribes and plot against the Europeans. The threat of slave rebellions and Indian attacks would be an ongoing concern among white settlers for years to come.

In 1731 Louisiana as a colony returned to the administration of the French King and a period of three decades of relatively stable commercial and social development followed. Sieur de Bienville replaced governor Perier in 1733 and with him returned relaxed relations with the local Indian tribes. New Orleans was still very much a frontier town with rudimentary wooden structures, a heavy fence surrounding it on three sides with the front side opening onto the river, and muddy, deep rutted roads laid out in a grid pattern with the same names as are found in the old part of the city today known as the French Quarter. The Ursulines, a French order of nuns, had arrived in 1727 and became well known during this period as hospital administrators and for their orphanage and their school for young girls. In fact, their Ursuline Academy continues today. The Ursulines, the Capuchins and other religious groups in Louisiana owned slaves throughout the colonial period and depended on them to maintain their convents, schools, asylums and churches. [1]

Living patterns were fluid and based more on convenience than race. Many families had a few slaves; others hired poor immigrants from France, Germany or Spain as domestics. Servants lived on the premises, usually in small extensions of the back of the main house. Slaves continued to do much of the physical labor involved in building the city, loading and unloading ships, digging drainage canals and constructing four forts, one at each corner of New Orleans. They also supplied much of the meat and fish for the city by fishing, hunting and trapping in the outlying swamps. Slaves and free blacks had access to the French Superior Council as evidenced by the 1748 cases of "Case of Infanticide by Negress Marie Jeanne" and "Murder Case against Baraca, a Negro slave of the King, in the killing of his wife Taca". [2]

Avenues to Freedom

It was during this thirty year span of rapid development in the city that a significant number of free blacks appeared and the term *les gens de couleur libre* or free people of color was first used. The term free black was also known, but it generally referred to a person of African descent recently freed, whereas free people of color meant those persons who were born into freedom, either as the second generation of free blacks in Louisiana or having entered the colony from the Caribbean as already free people. Not unlike the children of many immigrants of the time, they were quickly assimilated into the dominant French culture and felt themselves removed from the experience of their parents, that of slavery and an African identity.

Their parents had won their freedom through several channels; they had bought it, they had fought for it, or they had won it as a favor from a master or mistress. The black code allowed for slaves hiring themselves out or being hired out by their masters to perform all sorts of work in the city or in out-lying settlements. When a canal was to be dug, for example, or a large building constructed, hundreds of strong young slaves were required, drawing on the help of many privately owned Africans. This work was paid; most of the salary went to the master, but depending on the agreement between master and slave, a portion would be kept by the slave. Masters encour-aged their slaves to learn marketable skills and hire themselves out. This meant not only more income for the master but also greater incentive for slaves to work and support themselves. A frugal slave could eventually earn the price estimated to be his value and offer his master that amount for his freedom. Few slaves accomplished this in the French period, but the custom became fairly common during the Spanish reign. [3]

After the Natchez massacre of 1730-31 a number of slaves who had distinguished themselves on the side of the French troops were freed by the Crown as recognition of their service. The Indian wars of 1734-35 gave another opportunity for slaves to prove themselves useful in fighting indigenous tribes such as the Choctaw and thereby gaining freedom. In that

Typical housing arrangement in early New Orleans. Slaves lived upstairs in narrow building on left, an extension of the courtyard and main house where they worked. Stables and kitchen were located below.

protracted confrontation, over a hundred blacks fought with Bienville near Mobile in what is today Alabama. There were also several free men of color who served as military officers. One such captain, named Simeon or Simon, was given special honors by Bienville for his leadership and courage in battle. In 1739 Bienville with his French troops engaged in conflict against the Chickasaws near Memphis. His ranks contained

Indian allies such as the Choctaw – now allies – and 270 black soldiers from New Orleans, including a company of fifty free men of color, the rest slaves. The role of these soldiers of African descent was openly acknowledged by Bienville, and freedom, honor and privileges befitting any distinguished military men were their rewards.

The earliest record in Louisiana of a manumission procedure, or legal freeing of a slave by a master, was in 1733 when Bienville, the city's founder, freed his slaves Jorge and Marie who had served him for twenty-six years. This means they must have been in Bienville's household since 1707 when he lived in Mobile, well before the founding of New Orleans. It was common throughout the history of slavery in Louisiana for elderly slaves, who had served their masters well and were no longer able to work long hours, to be manumitted and allowed to live out their last years in freedom. There are also accounts during this period and under Spanish rule of a master or mistress upon his or her deathbed granting freedom to the family's slaves; in some cases the whole household was freed, in others only certain beloved ones were. Efforts were made to keep family units together: a slave woman usually received her children's freedom with her own, and slave spouses were often freed together.

African Market

Because food was in short supply during the 1730s and 1740s, slaves were encouraged to grow their own gardens and hunt and fish for their daily food. Frequent surpluses could be shared with others or more likely sold or traded at open air

Congo Square, formerly called Place des Negres, as it looks today.

markets. Although markets within the city walls were closely regulated, and most masters demanded an accounting of the sale of goods by slaves, an informal market system quickly developed. Beyond the rampart was an open plain or commons which by the 1740s took on the name Place des Negres because of the many Africans who gathered there on Sundays, their day off, to socialize and sell various fruits, vegetables, meats and other wares. This market operated outside city regulations and was probably a major source of private income for slaves as well as some free blacks. [4]

Whiling away the hours with their children at the Place

des Negres, African vendors of various tribes would dance and sing the songs and rhythms of their native towns. Soon tribal dancers, musicians and singers began competing in group performances, so that by the 1760s their market place was renamed Congo Square and drew spectators every Sunday from across the city. No other place in North America provided such a cultural haven for Africans in their early years of slavery nor gave them the opportunity to practice and preserve their native languages and customs.

This is not to say that slave life in New Orleans was idyllic; the large number of runaways attest to resistance to hard labor with little rest, malnutrition and abuse by masters. Others found life among the Indians or in their own small camps in the back swamps preferable to the regimentation of the master. The economy of the city was stagnant, causing difficulties for entrepreneurial slaves and free blacks. Few new slaves were brought to Louisiana in this period under the French because shipments direct from Africa had dwindled and slaves imported from the West Indies commanded high prices; therefore, the next generation of slaves had to come from a high birthrate among the slave women already in the city.

When Bienville retired to France in 1743 leaving the colony open to continued attacks by the Chickasaws, new French leadership had to deal with the complex society that had become New Orleans: whites were seriously outnumbered by non-whites, and a middle stratum of free people of color with ambition and know-how were poised to become the artisans and tradesmen on whom the city would depend.

An important point is made by Gwendolyn Midlo Hall in *Africans in Colonial Louisiana*, "...there is no evidence of the racial exclusiveness and contempt that characterizes more recent times ... no evidence that white settlers and French officials considered the Africans and their descendants uncivilized people." Survival for all racial groups was the preoccupation of the times, according to Hall's research. She sees the Africans in French Louisiana as "competent, desperately needed and far from powerless."

The Seven Years' War of France against England 1754-1763 meant even more severe economic restrictions on the French colony of Louisiana, while trade with France and other parts of Europe was cut off. The Peace of Paris, signed in 1763, gave Louisiana to Spain and opened a new era for the city of New Orleans.

The French Period 1731 - 1762

The Spanish Period 1763-1802

1763	Louisiana transferred from France to Spain
1764	First slave patrol organized to round up runaways
1769	O'Reilly finally establishes Spanish rule, minor changes in Black Code
1770s	Large number of free women of color acquire real estate in city
1771	Lebreton, Carrollton planter, killed by his personal slaves who are then hanged
1776	American Revolution: Spain neutral but New Orleans supports American rebels through its port
1778	Acadians and Isleños begin settling southern Louisiana
1779-81	Galvez's campaign against the British with help of free blacks
1782-84	Cimarron Wars: free blacks fight with Spanish to break up runaway slave groups.
1785-86	Spanish black code tightens for slave and free

1788-94	Two great fires destroy most of original city of New Orleans. Blacks do much of rebuilding
1789-95	French Revolution: all slaves in French West Indies set free. Haitian Revolution (1791-1804) establishes first independent black nation on continent of America
1795	Pointe Coupée Uprising: slaves and free blacks unite, march on New Orleans, quelled by militia
1796	Ban on all blacks entering Louisiana, black code made more restrictive for slave and free
1802	Spain nearly bankrupt, Louisiana returns to French rule

The Spanish Period 1763-1803

When French King Louis XV gave the colony of Louisiana to his cousin Spanish King Charles III in 1763 as a part of losing the Seven Years' War in Europe, the French citizens who had settled New Orleans and brought it through its infancy felt betrayed. The Louisiana Territory had been cut up and reduced to the land west of the Mississippi River as Spanish Louisiana, while Britain claimed the land to the east of the river as Florida. People on the west bank of the Mississippi, including New Orleans, would become subjects of the King of Spain which threatened their language, culture and customs.

For slaves and free people of color the change from French to Spanish rule posed problems of uncertainty as to how the Spanish black code and treatment of blacks would differ from those of their former rulers. They were gradually being cut off from trade and communication with family and friends in St. Domingue, the French colony in the West Indies, today called Haiti. With the death in 1758 of Markandal, a famous sorcerer and leader of runaway slaves in St. Domingue, blacks coming to Louisiana from that area were suspected of having learned the art of poisoning whites from Markandal. In 1763 a total ban on importation of slaves from St. Domingue was imposed. [1]

Resistance to the establishment of a Spanish regime in Louisiana was strong from the moment word of the change reached people there; open rebellion ensued. It took another six years for Spain to establish an orderly government in its

29

newly acquired colony in the person of an Irishman for hire to Spain, General Alejandro O'Reilly. Within months he had tracked down thirteen leaders of the French resistance and had them executed. Animosity between Spanish rulers and French Creoles marked the next thirty years.

Liberal Spanish Laws

O'Reilly also established new laws based on those of other Spanish colonies such as Cuba. *Las Partidas Siete*, dubbed O'Reilly's Code, contained several important new rules for slaves. The Spanish were reputed to be more liberal toward Africans than the French, and the new laws reflected that. Since some French families had returned to France or moved to the Caribbean without freeing their slaves, a slave could petition for freedom after living independent of his or her master for ten years. Slaves who became priests or who performed military and other integral services for the Spanish Crown were freed, as were slaves who had married free blacks. The right of *coartación* was introduced whereby freedom could be bought by a slave even when his master strenuously opposed the manumission. There were also rules forbidding mistreatment of slaves, even a law that afforded freedom to female slaves whose masters had hired them out as prostitutes. [2]

The Spanish period gave slaves and free people of color more security and rights than under any other regime. Free blacks were invited to serve in the militia, they could communicate openly with slaves and even buy and sell them. The 1778 census of New Orleans shows almost one-third of the free people of color owning at least one slave; in fact, a greater proportion of them owned slaves than did whites, and their treatment of slaves – as reflected in court cases or writers' observations of the time – were not markedly different than that of whites. Usually they had one or two slaves to help with the housekeeping and care of the children.

Free blacks were protected by law from arbitrary searches or ill treatment by the police. In Spain at the time there was no prohibition of interracial marriages, and although O'Reilly's Code forbade intermarriage of blacks and whites, the rules could be bent in cases of fair skinned mulattoes who passed for white. Many Spaniards with thick black hair and

St Louis Cathedral, built in 1794 and enlarged in 1851, was built with the help of slaves and free blacks. Slaves and later free people of color had to sit in the balcony.

ruddy complexions looked like brothers of creole blacks.

In his essay *The African Presence in Colonial Louisiana*, Thomas Fiehrer points out how the presence of "a large free colored class... made the total identification of blackness with slavery impossible." Slaves in Spanish Louisiana, he says, were often as not found running households, even entire estates, hunting to supply food, running errands, and spending time in taverns. Once free, they often continued a similar lifestyle. Fiehrer concludes, "The consummate linkage of negritude and servility, the dominant feature of race relations in the American Old South, never fully emerged in colonial Louisiana." [3]

The average free family of color, often headed by a single woman, had four to five members, and most free people of color lived alone with their children, whereas slave families were extensions of white households in which they served. There was a growth of direct African slave trade in Louisiana throughout the Spanish regime, infusing the area with a fresh African influence. Distinctions began to be made between Creole slaves, those who had been born in the West Indies or Louisiana, and Africans who had arrived directly from the homeland.

With improvement in commerce and business and opening the river to British as well as Spanish trading ships, people of all classes began to enjoy a more stable and prosperous life. Spanish was declared the official language, and business, law and journalism were bilingual, but French remained the standard language of the people. Customs, traditions and

Wrought iron to decorate balconies, fences, gates and tombs was commonly fashioned by slaves and free people of color who brought metallurgical science with them from Africa. Above: house in the French Quarter. Below: St. Louis Cemetery #2.

cuisine were only superficially influenced by the new rulers, who were primarily military officers assigned to Louisiana on a temporary basis. Those who married in New Orleans chose local French brides who in turn maintained French households. Some Spanish officers also consorted with free women of color, lending their Spanish surnames to the children from these unions who in turn could legally inherit one-tenth of their father's estate.

Free People of Color Form a Community

During the nearly forty years of Spanish rule two generations of children were born in New Orleans. Among the free people of color, population boomed and the decades of the 1760s through the 1790s saw many of them acquiring property, establishing businesses and becoming leaders in their social circle. In 1769 when O'Reilly arrived, there were 99 free people of color as heads of household out of a total 3,190 in New Orleans, a small percent. By the end of the Spanish rule in 1802, their numbers had risen to 1,355 out of a total of 8,050. Censuses and population counts during those years often did not include transients, of which there were many free blacks, nor mulattoes whose features and skin tones may have put them in the category of whites.

Notable too is the population imbalance between genders in New Orleans. Whereas white men of the period outnumbered white women by a small margin, free black women outnumbered free black men by two to one, and female slaves in general outnumbered male slaves. In addition, white men tended to outlive white women, but black women, whether slave or free, outlived black men. Work opportunities meant that many slave men were needed on plantations upriver and free black men moved to villages in rural Louisiana or migrated to the West Indies or to Europe. This left a large group of unmarried free women of color in the city with few prospects of marriage to free black men and the chance to have legitimate children. Marriage to a slave man could endanger the woman's freedom and was therefore not very common. [4]

Under these circumstances it is not surprising to learn that liaisons between free women of color and white men developed fairly frequently. As early as the 1730s there are records of young slave women given their freedom in New Orleans "in recognition of affection and services" to a master or because they were acknowledged as the daughters of French masters and slave mothers. French and Spanish explorers had long held the practice of taking as their mates indigenous and African women in colonial outposts throughout the Caribbean. Arriving in Louisiana, they continued the custom.

European men traditionally did not marry until their early thirties, and premarital relations with chaste and chaperoned white girls were unthinkable. It was accepted that white men in Louisiana would spend their youthful years in the company of a young black girl (age 12 to 15 was optimal) of their liking, to have children with her and to support, at least minimally, such families. For the wealthy planter or businessman, this liaison could often last a lifetime, regardless of an interim marriage to -- and family with -- a white woman. Not infrequently he chose never to marry, or if married would still shower his black lover with gifts and favors. From all indications, there was usually mutual affection between the black girl and her white suitor. This was a far different situation than the wanton raping by masters of slave women in other parts of the South. [5]

The Plaçage System: White Men, Black Concubines

Because the free woman of color living under the protection of a French or Spanish man was not technically his mistress nor was she a courtesan, which would have insinuated promiscuity, she was referred to in legal records of the time as a concubine and among her own community as a *placée*, from the French word placer, to place. During the Spanish period and on into the American regime, generations of free girls of color were raised with the expectation of some finding white protectors and rearing families by them. In their community such women were considered placed as the "wives" of white men, though their unions could not be legalized nor were there any written contracts. This informal social system gradually became known as *plaçage*; a woman placed with a white man was expected to be faithful to him until he either left her or died.

Plaçage in Louisiana was unique in North America and created an independence and power among free women of color that is only now being explored by scholars. How many women had such relationships is unknown; property records of the late 1760s through 1800 reveal dozens of free women of color who acquired prime real estate in New Orleans in their

Typical Creole cottage on Esplanade Avenue. Free women of color who had liaisons with white men were often given such houses and passed them to their children.

own names, had houses built and passed estates on to their children, who usually had surnames different from their mothers'. Court records up to the 1850s contain numerous successions–estate settlement–of white men, some of them top officials, where illegitimate children of color are acknowledged and given an inheritance from their fathers. Some of these men were lifelong bachelors with no legitimate heirs. Records at the St. Louis Church of New Orleans from 1782-1791 show 2,688 colored births but only 40 colored marriages, suggesting that the majority of the children were illegitimate, or "natural" children as the French called them, many presumably having white fathers. [6]

Marriage to a free man of color usually did not offer the same financial security to the woman, nor the privileges that lighter skinned children with Caucasian features would enjoy. Still there were always some free women of color who married free black men, some who had children with them out of wedlock, and others who had no children at all. By no means did all free women of color consort with white men.

Notorious among inter-racial families of the time was Don Jose Nicolas Vidal, acting civil governor for Spain, who came to Louisiana around 1780 and for whom the town of Vidalia is named. At his headquarters in New Orleans in the 1790s the free woman of color with whom he shared his home, Eufrosina Hisnard, was said to be in command. She screened his visitors and controlled his social calendar. She also bore him two daughters, who when his estate was settled in the early 1800s fought a lengthy court battle against Vidal's white children to procure their share of his wealth.

An example of this system in other parts of Louisiana is Marie Thereze or Coincoin (her African name), whose son Nicolas Augustin Metoyer was the patriarch of the large Cane River community of free people of color near Natchitoches, 260 miles northwest of New Orleans. Her more than 25-year liaison in the mid 1700s with a French official at the Natchitoches post, Claude Thomas Pierre Metoyer, in whose home she worked as a slave, resulted in ten children. Metoyer freed her in 1778, but she continued to serve him until his marriage ten years later with a French woman. Coincoin made a small fortune from tobacco farming on the 68 acres given her by Metoyer. In 1794 through Metoyer's influence she was granted a sizable piece of land from the King of Spain on which she developed a dairy. Her large estates on the Cane River and Red River were later divided among her progeny, and Yucca Plantation where in 1796 she built African House, the only African style building to survive in North America, later passed from her descendants to whites; renamed Melrose Plantation, it is open today for public tours. [7]

Naming Patterns

As people of color moved into the mainstream of the life and economy of New Orleans, they had to take on European names. African slaves under the French and Spanish were permitted to keep and use their native tribal names. They also were given Christian first names like Jean Baptiste or Marie Terese and frequently acquired a French or Spanish nickname like Pouponne, Manette or Ninon from their master. Upon being manumitted, a slave chose whatever name he or she wished to use officially but continued to be known by other names among family and friends. Colonial Louisiana records reflect many aliases for free blacks, and it is often difficult for researchers to determine which aliases match which persons and on what occasions which names were used. Variations in spelling and transposition of letters are additional problems.

A case in point: Marie Louisa appears to be the same woman in one record of the late 1700s as simply Louisa in another. A third reference has a Luisa Duconge which could

The African House, built by a free woman of color in Cane River, Louisiana in the early 1800s, is the only African style building to survive in North America.

be the same woman, while in a fourth record she appears as Luisa Gallaud alias Babet, possibly the same person as Marie L. Duconge alias Gallaud in a fifth record. Many free blacks appear to have taken on first names as surnames, because it is very common to see among them last names like Baptiste, Marie, Antoine, Pierre, Mathieu, Celestin(e), Etienne, and Francois, to name a few. Generally, illegitimate children of color were acknowledged by their white father and given his last name, but there are cases where it appears that only the white father's first or middle name was adopted. Sometimes too, the D' / Du or L' / La denoting rank in a white father's last name was dropped or a letter or two in the white man's surname was changed to denote his children of color. To this day some people of color in New Orleans have lifelong aliases; they are known by one name in intimate circles but have a completely different legal name. [8]

The Cimarron Wars: Runaway Slaves

The Spanish did not have enough manpower loyal to the Crown to defend the large Louisiana Territory in Indian skirmishes and incursions by the British to the east on the one hand, and at the same time enforce their laws among rebellious African slaves and insolent French and Creole planters on the other. They depended on a third group, the free men of color, to serve as a slave patrol. Two companies of free black militia who had fought under Governor Bernardo de Galvez during the 1770s to rout the British from the lower Mississippi River region during the American Revolution were soon pressed into service back in New Orleans. They manned the forts and walls around the city controlling the traffic in and out, checking for fugitive slaves, and enforcing curfews.

Frequently they were sent on expeditions to outlying plantations to scout for problems, pursue runaway slaves and report back to the governor. By the early 1780s escaped slaves, called marones or maroons or cimarrons by the Spanish, had established their own armed communities in the cypress swamps surrounding the city and rural plantations. The maroon camps were supported with food and other goods given them by indigenous tribes, working slaves, or stolen at night on raids of former masters. Whole slave families deserted together through a maze of secret pathways, and eked out a living in crudely fashioned huts. Some camps had developed as early as the 1750s when slaves worked cutting and hauling cypress logs for local sawmills. These slaves were accustomed to living and traveling in the dense swamps. Despite harsh penalties if caught, many slaves defied abusive masters and stayed marooned for years at a time. [9]

Slave rebellions were a constant concern of whites who on remote plantations were greatly outnumbered by Africans. In 1771 the murder of a master Lebreton by his personal servants on his Carrollton plantation a few miles above New Orleans caused a general panic. Long after the slaves were hanged for their misdeeds, fear prevailed. From 1782 to 1784 the Spanish army joined forces with the free men of color and waged war on the cimarron camps. Jean St. Malo, the famed rebel slave leader, fought to the bitter end but was eventually captured and executed. The legends of slave renegade Bras Coupé that flavored Louisiana story telling for years to come are believed based on St. Malo's heroic feats. Although the campaign to rout the cimarrons and destroy their camps cost a number of slaves' lives, it by no means brought an end to runaways nor the threat they posed; the cimarron system continued into the1850s.

A new governor, Esteban Miro, arrived in 1785 and tightened the Black Code to give him more control over the fairly lax standards of non-whites. Sometimes dubbed the Tignon Law, the general restrictions imposed by Miro outlawed the sale of alcohol to people of color, prohibited labor on Sundays, and restricted travel of slaves. Masking by blacks at dances and balls had been prohibited in 1781, and now public meetings and dancing among people of color was permitted only in Place des Negres, later called Congo Square, which still lay outside the city's walls.

Apparently free women of color had become a threat to white women, for Miro also commanded that no hats be worn in public by free black women, and that these women be encouraged to make their own living rather than act as "libertines". Because no woman could appear in public in those days with her head uncovered, the free black women had to resort to the kerchiefs worn by slave women; their ingenuity, however, prevailed and in no time they appeared in the streets with colorful madras scarves wrapped high on their heads in elegant turban or *tignon* style trimmed with feathers and gems. [10,] See photo p. 45.

In both 1788 and 1794 fires raged through New Orleans; each time many blocks of wooden buildings and houses were destroyed. The Spanish relied heavily on slave labor and the engineering and building skills of blacks, both slave and free, to rebuild the city. These construction projects drew black workers from other parts of Louisiana as well.

Pointe Coupée Uprising

At the end of the century with the French Revolution brewing in Europe and word of a massive slave insurrection growing in St. Domingue in the Caribbean, Spain felt itself beleaguered in Louisiana. The Pointe Coupée uprising was about to bring even more chaos. In rural, isolated outposts of the Territory a frontier mentality prevailed. Rules were made and enforced on a local level.   In times when food was scarce and conditions harsh, animosities quickly formed between African slaves divided into tribal groups and the light skinned mulattoes and other free blacks who supervised them. Louisiana slaves were well aware of the French Revolution and the probability that with the fall of the monarchy to the ideals of equality for all, slaves throughout the French colonies would be given their freedom. That the Spanish would follow suit was doubtful. [11]

In 1795 a large group of slaves on the plantation of Julian Poydras in Pointe Coupée Parish, about a hundred miles upriver from New Orleans, formed a sophisticated plan to kill their masters and abolish slavery in Louisiana. There had been a series of incidents of unrest preceding the actual attempt.   In April several white sympathizers and some of the most trusted free blacks in the area colluded with the Poydras slaves, led by Antoine Sarrasin, to initiate a massacre of local planters. While Poydras was gone on a business trip, the slaves came close to setting a building on fire as a distraction to break into the ammunition store and begin their rampage south to New Orleans. However, the plot was betrayed by the Tunica Indians, and fifty blacks were captured and convicted of conspiracy. Twenty-three slaves were hanged and their white co-conspirators exiled from Louisiana. Heads of the slaves were displayed on poles along the Mississippi River to warn anyone else contemplating resistance. But more slave plots were discovered in the next months, and whites throughout the colony

Portrait of an unidentified free woman of color by Antoine Collas circa 1820. The original hangs in the New Orleans Museum of Art. Note the tignon headdress worn by such women of the time. Photo courtesy of the New Orleans Historic Voodoo Museum.

lived in a state of panic.

The eighteenth century in Louisiana closed on a very troubled note. Europe was fraught with internal wars, the Americans were quickly moving into the lower Mississippi region, many Frenchmen clamored for Louisiana to be returned to France, and the freedom of all slaves and full civil rights for people of color in the Caribbean caused extreme unrest among Louisiana blacks. Something would have to give and soon.

Louisiana Purchase and
Early American Years 1803-1830

1800	Napoleon forces Spain to return Louisiana to France
1803	Napoleon sells Louisiana to the United States
1803-10	Influx of black refugees from St. Domingue (Haiti) to New Orleans
1804	Free black property owners plan to petition Congress for right to vote
1805	First quadroon ball recorded
1807	Faubourg Marigny opens to development.
1811	St. John slave revolt upriver heads toward N.O. Dozens of slaves killed
1815	Battle of New Orleans: free men of color decisive in Andrew Jackson's victory
1813-30	Golden Age of free people of color in Louisiana
1830	Repressive laws passed to restrict free people of color in the state

Louisiana Purchase and
Early American Years 1803-1830

When U.S. President Thomas Jefferson purchased Louisiana for $15 million from France in 1803, the majority of people in New Orleans were African or of African descent. The census figure quoted by most historians is that out of a total population of 8,050, well over half were of color: 2,775 slaves and 1,335 free people of color. There probably was an undercount of the latter group, since by that time a number of third and fourth generation free blacks had assumed a white Creole identity.

The first American governor, Virginian W.C.C. Claiborne, was hardly prepared for the assertive community of well to do free people of color, many of whom had never known slavery but rather owned slaves themselves; they wore military uniforms, were armed, and claimed French parentage. The new rulers also looked askance at the ease with which white, slave and free black associated, the independence of many slaves, their lack of a servile manner, and their dancing and socializing in the streets of the city. Property records reveal that in 1803 more than a quarter of houses and estates along the main streets of the city were owned by free blacks, the large majority of them single women. All this spelled decadence to the statesmen from other parts of the South where British laws and Puritanical ideals viewed slaves as mere chattel and severely restricted the freeing of Africans. [1]

The transition from a French-Spanish colony to part of

the vast United States of America was difficult for New Orleanians, especially for free people of color who were subject to a less tolerant and even vindictive attitude from the new rulers. But they were too influential as a community of color, too wealthy and too well connected with whites to be driven into a subservient position. Many chose to leave rather than submit to the Americans, while many others chose to stay and assert their rights.

Restrictions for People of Color

The Haitian Revolution from 1791 to 1804, led by free black Toussaint L'Ouverture with strong ties to New Orleans, caused thousands of free people of color and slaves with their Creole masters to pour into the city in the years following the

Joseph Forneret, a watchmaker and prosperous free man of color, acquired this house at 401 Dauphine Street and many other properties around it in the French Quarter in the late 1700s. Some remained with his heirs until the 1870s.

49

Purchase. Over 3,000 free blacks entered the state between 1809 and 1810 alone. Claiborne could do little to curtail this immigration but began imposing restrictions on the movements and behavior of people of color whose population in Louisiana had nearly doubled by 1810. Free men of color from St. Domingue or Haiti above age fifteen were asked to leave Louisiana.

All free blacks were required to carry proof of their freedom, which was an insult to people who had never known slavery. Whenever their names appeared in public records, they had to be followed by the notation f.m.c. or f.w.c. (free man or woman of color) to distinguish them from whites. In French records the notation was h.c.l. or f.c.l. *(homme or femme de couleur libre)*. Both slave and free blacks had to observe the nine o'clock nightly curfew, and permission was required for them to leave the city and visit family members or travel on business in other parts of the state. In order to be freed, a slave had to be thirty years or older and have served his or her master faithfully for at least four years. [2]

As noted before, similar attempts had been made to control people of color under the Spanish regime but met with only limited success. Slave revolts proved to be an ongoing threat, no matter who occupied the governor's house. Most notorious of these was the 1811 St. John slave revolt, believed to be the largest in U.S. history. Hundreds of slaves in St. James and St. John the Baptist parishes, led by Haitian slave Charles Deslonde, began a carefully planned march January 18, 1811 from Woodland Plantation – today in the town of LaPlace – 35 miles northwest of New Orleans. As they passed various plantations along the River Road, killing several owners, their ranks swelled to over 500. Armed with machetes, axes and stolen guns, they chanted "*Allons a la Nouvelle Orléans!*" where they hoped to seize the arsenal and overthrow the American government. Two days later and ten miles upriver from their intended mark, the unruly mob was stopped in a bloody battle with white planters and militia. Over 60 slaves were killed and 75 captured; after a trial at nearby Destrehan Plantation, 36 slaves were executed and their heads hung on posts along the river to warn would-be rebels. Though later overshadowed in national slave history by the uprisings led by Denmark Vesey 1822 and Nat Turner 1831, which the St. John group influenced, this local revolt that came close to changing the state's history is commemorated in an historical marker in LaPlace along LA 61. [3]

In New Orleans enforcement of segregation of whites and blacks was almost impossible because of the close blood ties and intimate living arrangements. The French and white Creoles who had lived for generations in colonial Louisiana, had little respect for *les americains*, who spoke no French, ignored the great cultural traditions of the French opera and theater in New Orleans, and in general conducted themselves as barbarians, according to French sensitivity. The original city became the refuge of the colonial past and the white Creoles and free people of color, while the American intruders set up their own city hall, police force, businesses and Protestant churches farther up river in a separate area called Lafayette. Gallier Hall, Lafayette Park and Lafayette Cemetery in uptown New Orleans are reminders today of the early American separation that lasted into mid-century.

Golden Age of the Free People of Color

Many free blacks reacted to the affront of American repression by selling their properties and emigrating to Paris where some already had relatives and investments, or by traveling west to unexplored Indian or Spanish territories. People of mixed Indian, African and French blood could blend in with the sparse populations of these wide open areas or form communities of free black emigres, as they did in Vera Cruz, Mexico. [4] Others were lured to stay on in the city because of rapid economic development from which they were well positioned to benefit. Indeed, the two decades from 1813 to the early 1830s are considered by researchers as the Golden Age of the free people of color in New Orleans. The suburbs or *faubourgs* as the French called them, of Marigny in 1807 and Tremé in 1812 were developed from old plantations to offer housing to an overflow of families from the Creole city. Many free people of color purchased small plots of land there and built modest homes side by side with whites. [5]

By the mid-1830s free blacks owned $2.5 million in property in New Orleans. They had their own schools, usually operated as small, private institutions in educators' homes. The earliest recorded school was in 1813 operated by G. Dorefeuille, a free man of color. Some of the young men and women were sent to France or schools in northern United States to be educated. At the French opera and theater they had their box seats in the second tier, on Sundays they attended mass at the St. Louis Cathedral, and throughout the week they kept a busy social schedule of balls, parties and meetings of benevolent groups. They acted in the first theater, founded in 1793 by

Madame Derosier of St. Domingue, attended traveling circuses, and took an avid interest in the dramatic and musical arts of the city.

The free men of color were intensely political. As early as 1804 those who owned property had proposed a petition to be delivered to Washington asking that free black property-owning men be given the right to vote on tax issues. The plan was dis-

Madam John's Legacy is the name of a famous French Quarter landmark, as the plaque attests. In the story "Tite Poulette" by George W. Cable set in the 1820s, a fictitous free woman of color inherited this house built in the West Indies style.

covered by local whites and quickly squelched as inflammatory, but it was the beginning of a long and ardent struggle for self determination and inclusion in American politics. *L'Abeille* or The Bee, a newspaper founded in New Orleans in 1827 by Creole whites from Haiti, had a progressive editorial stance toward race. Several free blacks, using pen names as was the custom of the day, reportedly contributed to its pages.

White refugees from St. Domingue allied themselves with free blacks in other ways. In 1805 one named Grandjean organized slaves and free men of color in New Orleans to revolt against the Americans. Their plot was foiled by several free men of color who were rewarded with large cash sums, while Grandjean and his accomplices were sentenced to work on a slave chain gang for life. [6]

Trades and Avocations

Not all free people of color were well off; the majority appear to have earned a modest income from trades, work as artisans, vending routes, small shops and prudent investments from inheritances. In many cases they worked alongside slaves or employed them. They lived in close knit families, were devout Catholics, and rarely appeared in police records. Gradually they dominated the leather working trade in the city, making the harnesses, valises and shoes, suspenders, and belts essential to city life. As clothiers, their tailoring and dressmaking skills were sought out by rich Creole and American clients alike.

Renowned as cigar-makers, wood workers, ironworkers, marble sculptors, masons, builders and stone cutters, they supplied much of the labor and materials for mansions, public buildings, and monumental tombs, which today continue to attract visitors to New Orleans, Much of the original hand wrought iron for lamp braces, hinges and locks as well as the graceful lines of decorative balcony railings, fences and gates was fashioned by them as blacksmiths and ironworkers. As draymen and liverymen they were licensed to operate horse stables and carts and carriages.

They appear in city directories of the period as shop owners, carpenters, coopers, wigmakers, laundresses and many other professions. They peddled fruits, vegetables, candies and cakes throughout the city; some of the women, led by Rose Nicaud, introduced the sale of hot coffee at the markets. Other women worked as private hairdressers, and seamstresses for wealthy ladies, dressing them for elegant parties, while still others opened small eating houses or offered planters traveling into the city on business a room for the night and a hot meal. They applied age old herbal recipes and natural healing techniques to nursing the sick of all races. [7]

This period saw the birth and education of free men and women of color in New Orleans who were to become famous during the boom years of the city into the mid-and-later-1800s. For example, Robert Norbert Rillieux (1806-1894), son of the Frenchman Vincent Rillieux and free woman of color Constance Vivant, started out as a successful young blacksmith and became an expert machinist, inventing the pan method of processing sugar which revolutionized the sugar industry in Louisiana. Daniel and Eugene Warbourg born in the 1820s of Daniel Warbourg, a wealthy German-Jewish real estate speculator, and his slave Marie Rose Blondeau whom he later freed, studied sculpture with French teachers and had their own shop of marble cutting, tombs and statuary. Marie Laveau (1783-1881), born of the French Laveau-Trudeau family and Marguerite Darcantel, a mother of color, began practicing voodoo rituals about the time of the Louisiana Purchase and taught her daughter, also named Marie Laveau (1827-1897), who succeeded her as voodoo queen. [8] Composers such as Edmond Dédé and Basile Bares, writers like Victor Sejour, and journalists of color like Armand Lanusse, many of whom studied in France and became well known in the 1850s, formed their earliest impressions during these chaotic years.

The Battle of New Orleans

In contrast to repressive laws by the Americans and restrictions on the rights of the free people of color, the military welcomed them and treated them like whites. State legislators had tried to reduce the large number of black soldiers and officers, but General Andrew Jackson, facing a protracted campaign against the British in the Gulf of Mexico, sought out the help of experienced free black troops who had proven themselves repeatedly in rounding up and controlling run-away slaves and repelling Indian skirmishes.

In 1812 Andrew Jackson enlisted two battalions of free men of color and in an official proclamation declared them equal to whites in the benefits their military service would earn them:

Opposite: Portrait of a young free woman of color by an unknown artist. The subject is believed to be Marie Laveau, hairdresser by profession, voodoo queen by religious calling. Photo courtesy of the New Orleans Historic Voodoo Museum.

equal pay ($124), rations, uniforms and bounty money. Plus, he offered them each 160 acres of land. Colonel Joseph Savary, free man of color, was appointed captain of the black troops. Jackson must have been sure of his need for the expertise and loyalty of these men, since his white superiors expressed severe disapproval at the level to which he had raised the free black soldiers. They seriously doubted the loyalty of men they did not even consider American citizens. [9]

But Jackson's judgment paid off in the last days of December 1814 and the early days of 1815 when the free men of color, numbering more than six hundred, became crucial in the victory over the British in the Battle of New Orleans. The American troops engaged the British in a series of confrontations a few miles downriver from the city that culminated in fierce fighting at the Chalmette Battleground, January 8, 1815. The colored battalions sustained many injuries and a few casualties, though exact figures have not survived. Jackson himself stated in a letter to the Secretary of War that the fatal shot that felled the British leader in the battle, General Sir Edward Pakenham, "I have always believed [was] the bullet of a free man of color, who was a famous rifle shot." Jordan Noble, a fourteen year old black boy, drummed orders throughout the battle, and free women of color helped nurse the wounded in makeshift hospital tents.

Although honored by Jackson after the battle and acknowledged as veterans with modest pensions along with whites, the free soldiers of color never received full citizenship nor the land and privileges they had been promised. But black soldiers marched along with white during the annual anniversary celebrations of the Battle of New Orleans years thereafter, and their military service gave them and their families status in the city and general benefits in the eyes of state government.

Quadroon Balls

Much is made in local histories of the quadroon balls, dances held for the purpose of introducing young white men to free women of color. The mothers of the young black girls attended these balls as well, and reportedly entered into elaborate verbal contracts with their daughters' prospective suitors. The white man had to prove he would be able to support the young woman, usually age 14-16, and take care of their children, before the mother would place her daughter officially under the man's protection.

The earliest recorded ball of this type appears in 1805. Although free men of color were often hired to play music at such events, they were not allowed to participate in the dance. White women were also prohibited, although there are a few references to masked wives, fiancés, or mothers of some of the white men sneaking into the balls to determine who was in attendance. [10]

Why these dances were dubbed quadroon balls is not certain. Not all free women of color attending had one fourth black blood (white grandfather and also white father, which was the official definition of a quadroon). Some had one-eighth (white great-grandfather, grandfather and father) and would have been known as octoroons, while others were fairly dark skinned. However, in literature of the times, written exclusively by white men, it appears that all light complexioned free women of color with European features were referred to as quadroons.

How often and where these dances were held is also not well recorded. They appear to have continued on a fairly regular basis into the 1850s and were noted by northern and foreign travelers as one of the novelties of a trip to New Orleans. Historically, the hotel at 717 Orleans Street that is said today to have held quadroon balls did not do so, but such balls are recorded as having occurred a few doors up the block at the

The Orleans Ballroom in the French Quarter is part of local lore as a site where quadroon balls reportedly were held and white men courted free women of color. It also later housed the convent of a religious order of free women of color (see page 72).

comer of Bourbon Street at the Davis Dance Hall in a building that no longer exists. [11]

Balls were extremely popular among all sectors of the city, so a dance designed to bring young free women of color together with prospective white suitors was not so unusual. By all accounts, the young women of color were lavishly attired and good dancers. This social occasion gave both the young women and their male counterparts an opportunity to get to know each other and to find mutual attractions. Not all liaisons between these two groups developed out of such balls, but doubtless a good many of them did.

The quadroon balls were also a way for American men to meet free women of color. Under the French and Spanish regimes, whites and free blacks had fairly fluid social and living patterns which made interacting quite natural. After 1803 the Americans imposed their own disapproval of any race mixing or miscegenation. However, once the quadroon balls became an institution in the Creole part of the city, many American men found it within their consciences to surreptitiously attend them; some even had families with free women of color, much like the white Creole men did. Interestingly, the mystique of the tragic quadroon heroine to whom white men are fatally attracted but whom they can never marry makes its way into American literature around this same time. [12]

As the 1830s dawned, another era of repressive laws for the free people of color in New Orleans was beginning. Northern Protestant and abolitionist forces were infiltrating the city calling on free blacks to organize in solidarity with slaves against the government. The American Colonization Society was actively repatriating freed slaves back to Africa. Once again, hundreds of free people of color prepared to leave the city of their birth and find their futures in France, the American West or Mexico.

Antebellum Years 1830-1860

1830	Laws passed to control blacks, limiting freedom of speech, emancipation of slaves and right to remain in Louisiana
1833	Streetcar for whites is attacked by blacks protesting lack of public transportation
1837	Death of Madame Couvent, ex-slave whose estate established first major school for children of color in 1848
1837	Several slave rebellions foiled
1837	Panic of 1837: nationwide financial crisis as banks fail. Many free people of color lose their properties
1840s	Local press first takes notice of voodoo in New Orleans, practitioners raided and arrested
1842	Founding of Sisters of the Holy Family in New Orleans, Catholic order of free black nuns
1843	L'Album Litteraire publishes literary works of free men of color
1844	Des Artisens founded, first social aid and pleasure club for blacks

1845	Les Cenelles, first and only collection of poetry by free men of color in U.S. published in New Orleans
1850	John McDonogh dies, end of his program to send hundreds of his freed slaves to Liberia, Africa
1852	End of Creole rule in New Orleans. City unites under American jurisdiction. New harsh laws against free blacks, many return to Haiti
1853	Most severe yellow fever epidemic claims 10,000 lives in city. Free women of color serve as nurses
1860	Dawn of the Civil War

Antebellum Years 1830-1860

The mention of antebellum New Orleans evokes idyllic images of women in bonnets and hooped skirts, splendid plantation homes built from fortunes made from cotton and sugar, and steamboats chugging slowly on the river: New Orleans as Queen of the South, a great commercial center. This is the conventional view of the unprecedented boom years that brought fame and fortune to what had been a fairly isolated and unremarkable settlement along the Mississippi. However, this view leaves out a large part of the population. New Orleans during those years was also the most important slave market in the United States, and vast estates of the era depended on the cheap and available labor of Africans. The antebellum years brought harsh and repressive laws for the slaves and free people of color. Many resisted in ill-fated rebellions, many others chose to leave the city forever, and a few free families of color cultivated their ties to whites and actually prospered.

In 1830 two major laws were passed to closely control the expanding influence and population of free blacks in Louisiana. Both were predicated on the fact that no person of African descent was a U.S. citizen but rather a subject of the ruling government of the time. There was also concern over the fact that at the time 735 free people of color in New Orleans owned 2,351 slaves, many of them family members or friends who would be freed. The first law was designed to discourage emancipation of slaves. Owners had to post a $1000 bond to guarantee that any freed slave would leave the state within thirty days after being manumitted. Free blacks from other parts of the country were prohibited from entering the state unless for exceptional reasons. Those who had entered Louisiana after statehood in 1812 were required to register with the government or else leave the state within sixty days. Furthermore, proof of freedom had to be carried by all free people of color at all times.

The second law prohibited the press from printing articles favorable to slaves and free blacks. Protest and discontent on the part of blacks was not to be published, and the right to assemble was curtailed. Blacks could no longer testify against whites in court. In addition, slaves could not be educated. [1]

For those who had been free for generations and who had never experienced slavery, such regulations were insulting and demeaning. To slaves who had anticipated gaining their freedom soon or having free family members buy them and manumit them, the future looked especially bleak. At first the new laws were disregarded by the majority of people, black and white, who had existed for decades in a liberal and mutually beneficial state, but in 1842 an act forcing recently arrived free blacks to leave Louisiana and cutting off contact with the West Indies sent people of color into an uproar. The population of free people of color plummeted from 19,000 in 1840 to 10,000 in 1850 as anyone who could liquidate local assets and leave for France and other parts of Europe or Mexico did so. Property records show hundreds of houses owned by people of color were sold during the 1830s and 1840s. Discrimination was evident in banks and lending institutions; for example, the Citizens Bank of New Orleans, which in 1833 refused to sell stocks to free people of color out of fear that they were numerous and wealthy enough to take over the bank. The national bank failure and financial panic of 1837 added to the pressure on many free blacks to sell large pieces of property that had been in their families for generations [2]

A large slave revolt in Virginia in 1831 led by Nat Turner caused unrest among the local population, and throughout the 1830s there were various forms of insurrection resulting in the hanging of leaders both slave and free. There were open protests against issues like blacks being refused transportation by streetcar to the lake. Anger and distrust festered beneath the surface of city life.

Accomplishments despite Barriers

Remarkably, the community of free people of color survived intact throughout the difficult years preceding the Civil War. Doubtless this was due in part to strong family support systems and close ties with whites. Many free blacks, according to city directories of those years, appear to have continued working in their trades as masons, builders, leather workers, etc., although in many cases they had to compete against ever increasing cheap immigrant labor. They hired on to major city projects like the digging of the New Basin Canal in the 1830s and held on to well established shops and clientele in the old part of the city. Eighty per cent of them were literate, and most sent their children to school. [3]

They had an active social and cultural life, in rare cases joining with free blacks who had moved into the city from other states; since these people spoke no French or Creole, language and customs must have been a problem. The Negro Philharmonic Society had over one hundred members in those years,

1915 graduating class of Straight University in New Orleans. Students represent variety of Creole families that date back to the 1700s. Photo courtesy of Amistad Research Center.

and a theater for black performers and black audiences was authorized in 1838. Des Artisens, a precursor to the social aid and pleasure clubs still active among blacks in New Orleans, was formed in 1844. A year earlier the radical *L'Album Litteraire*, a periodical founded by Frenchman J.L. Marciacq and free man of color Armand Lanusse, had printed the essays and poetry of black intellectuals. Although it lasted less than a year, it inspired *Les Cenelles, choix de poesies indigenes* in 1845, a collection of eighty-five poems by seventeen free men of color, among them Camille Thierry, Victor Sejour, Pierre Dalcour, Mirtil Ferdinand Liotau, and Joanni Questi.

The poems were traditional French verse about love,

death, and religion; there was almost nothing to indicate that the poets were black.

Lanusse, the editor, featured his own lengthy memorial poem to his brother Numa Lanusse, also a poet, who died at age 26. Copies of this limited edition work are very rare today; it was even more rare at the time in the United States for the descendants of slaves to be writing and publishing their own literature. [4]

Nor were such men apolitical. In 1838, led by Jean Fleming, they presented a petition for the right of property-owning free men of color to vote in state elections but were rejected in the state House of Representatives. In 1844 those light skinned enough to pass for white formed the Clay Club to vote in a national election for pro-slavery presidential candidate Henry Clay because of his support of the sugar interests; several were able to vote without being disqualified. In 1853 those who had fought in the Battle of New Orleans formed the Association of Colored Veterans to keep visible the presence of black soldiers in the parades and celebrations of the war. [5]

Thriving Businessmen and Professionals

Some free black businessmen and entrepreneurs did very well during these boom years. Etienne Cordeviolle and Francois Lacroix had a large clothier business and also were wealthy real estate developers. Both had inherited valuable properties from their mothers of color, Maria Del Rosario and Elizabeth Norwood respectively. Lengthy liaisons with their sons' white fathers, Estevan Cordeviola (Italian) and Paul Lacroix (French), had yielded these women estates that they then passed on to their heirs.

Similarly Julien Colvis (sometimes spelled Clovis) and Joseph Dumas, also tailors and real estate speculators, descended from French army officers and mulatto women in St. Domingue. Their mothers passed on to them properties in New Orleans and France. By the 1840s the tailor business of Colvis & Dumas at 124 Chartres Street was doing very well, and the young men divided their time between business interests in Louisiana and Paris, where Dumas is believed to have been related to the French novelist Alexandre Dumas who had a similar birthright. Colvis' son Joseph married Joseph Dumas' daughter Marguerite Dumas in 1869, joining two powerful estates. They lived with the three Colvis daughters in France where they were accepted as white. [6]

Another successful tailor business was operated in the 1830s by the Legoaster brothers, Philipe Aime and Erasme Gilbert. Their grandfather was Frenchman Giles Legoaster, and their father Erasme Gilbert Legoaster, born to Giles' slave Manon, had married Elisabeth Aimeé Gaillard of a wealthy family of color. The brothers had large estates in New Orleans and Paris. In 1850 Philippe Aime reported his taxable property in New Orleans as $150,000, one of the largest estates of free people of color. However, they left few progeny. Their sister, Aimée Legoaster, owned much of the 800 block of Dauphine Street, which in 1924 was donated to the Lafon Asylum for children of color. The Louisanna Legoaster name died out in Paris in 1955.

D. Mercier & Sons Emporium of Fashion and Fair Dealing developed out of a shoe business at Dauphine and Bienville streets in the mid-1800s. Dominique Mercier, free man of color who had a plantation near the city, built up the clothing business with his sons Joseph Anselme, Jean Leopold and William J. After the Civil War Mercier Realty and investments, operated by his sons, was a major factor in real estate dealings in the city.

There are many more names of free men of color who inherited property from their families and parlayed it into successful businesses during this period. Of course, some were not as fortunate, and their names show up on bankruptcy records. Noel Carriere and Barthelemy Campanel both inherited parts of their white fathers' estates and became real estate moguls, while Drausin Barthelemy Macarty is credited with having bought $56,081 worth of real estate and sold $50,355 in properties in the decade 1849-1859. Cecée Macarty, possibly Drausin's sister Celeste, inherited $12,000 from her mother Henriette Prieto and built up an importing business that by her death in 1845 was worth $155,000. She was also listed as the largest slave holder among the free people of color. Reported to have unlimited credit throughout Louisiana, she also did note discounting as a side business. [7]

Pierre A.D. Casenave was the clerk of an importing business of Judah P. Touro, a wealthy Jewish merchant in New Orleans. As executor and beneficiary of Touro's estate in 1854, Casenave received $10,000. He opened several mortician businesses which his descendants continue to operate today. Lucien Mansion and his nephew Georges Alces dominated the cigar industry in New Orleans in the mid-1800s, employing hundreds of workers. Their close ties with Haiti and Cuba served them

well in procuring the finest tobaccos. Families like the Dolli-
oles (Joseph, Jean-Luis and Pierre), the Porches and Lamottes
(Andre Martain) amassed fortunes as contractors and builders.
Louis Nelson Fouché was a mathematician and architect who
designed many houses in the Tremé section and worked with
his relative Dutre or Dutreuil Fouchér, a ship broker. Thomy
Lafon owned a major shoe store which his sister Alphée Baudin
operated while he attended to a growing real estate business.

Arthur Esteves had one of the largest sail-making businesses in the South. Beatrix Chenau was the lone free woman
of color who operated as a trader in the 1830s. Bazile Crocker,
famous fencing instructor, had his own school, and there were
physicians Oscar Guimbilotte, Francois Ruiz Alpuente and John
Chaumette, dentist P.A. Snaer, and pharmacist Albert Bowman.
Even the keeper of the cathedral in 1852 was a free man of
color, Joseph M. Cam.

Couvent School and Sisters of the Holy Family

When Madame Marie Justine Ciraire Couvent, who
had been brought to Louisiana as a slave from Africa, died a
wealthy free woman in 1837, it took another ten years to have
her succession processed. Couvent and her husband had been
devoted to the Ursuline nuns, even taking on the name Couvent (convent) as their surname. As a childless widow, Couvent
willed her estate to establishing a school for children of color,
but whites strongly opposing the education of such children,
blocked access to the money for a decade. With financial back-
ing of free black philanthropists like Aristide Mary, Francois
LaCroix and Thomy Lafon, a committee of free men of color
was able to finally probate Couvent's will and open the Institu-

St. Mary's Academy, now at 6901 Chef Menteur Highway, has educated women of color in New Orleans since 1867. It is operated by the Sisters of the Holy Family.

Plaque on 717 Orleans Street in the French Quarter indicates this was the site of the Sisters of the Holy Family until 1964. The order was founded in 1842 by free woman of color Heneriette DeLille, whom the vatican is considering for sainthood. See building page 60)

tion Catholique des Orphelins Indigents in 1847.[8]

It was administered and staffed by the brightest and best of the free black community. Several teachers were women as was one of the principals, Felicie Callioux. Writers Armand Lanusse, Joanni Questi and Paul Trevigne also served as principals of the school at various times. Many of the school's early students became business and political leaders after the Civil War. The school, later known as St. Louis School of Holy Redeemer, closed in 1994. There was also a public school, the Marie C. Couvent School, from 1939 to 1994, when it was changed to A. P. Tureaud School. Since Couvent was a slave owner, Tureaud was chosen as a more recent and positive black role model for children attending the school. In a time when free people of color owned much property in New Orleans and paid heavy taxes but were not permitted to send their children to public schools, having control of their own private institution of education was essential.

In the area of religion free women of color distinguished themselves in 1842 by founding the Congregation of the Sisters of the Holy Family, their own Catholic order. Convents were closed to blacks, so for Henriette DeLille, daughter of the white merchant Jean Baptiste Delille Sarpy and free woman of color Marie Joseph (alias Pouponne) Dias to fulfill her dream of becoming a nun, she had to procure the assistance of a white woman, Marie Jean Aliquot. Along with two other free women of color, Juliette Gaudin and Josephine Charles, Delille was able to get the order affiliated and open a church, school and orphanage in the 700 block of Orleans Street in a building donated by her relative, a wealthy free man of color, Thomy

Lafon. The order moved in the 1960s to Chef Menteur Highway where they continue to staff the Lafon Home, a home for the elderly, founded in 1848 and a girls' secondary school, St. Mary's Academy, founded in 1867.[9]

The McDonogh Connection

John McDonogh (1779-1850), a wealthy American planter from Baltimore who owned vast properties in New Orleans, is remembered primarily for his large bequest on his death in 1850 to establish a public school system in the city. A number of those schools in New Orleans continue to bear his name today, and once a year school children honor him by placing flowers at his statue near City Hall. But for people of African descent McDonogh had a different legacy. He was a founder of the American Colonization Society, a national organization to establish a homeland for freed slaves outside the South where they could govern themselves, maintain their native culture and live truly free of white domination. The Society looked first at land in the American northwest but settled eventually on a large tract of land in West Africa which was named Liberia. A capital city was established, and the condition for some American slaves was that they agree to be repatriated there upon being freed. McDonogh led the society's efforts in New Orleans. From his immense fortunes, he gave generously to the establishment of Liberia as an African nation, and he educated dozens of his own slaves working to earn their freedom and to replace themselves with other slaves. An example is Washington Watts McDonogh, whom his master supported for three years at Lafayette College in Pennsylvania in the 1830s. The young man went to Liberia as a Presbyterian missionary in

1843 and served there until 1871.[10]

McDonogh had a large plantation in Algiers across the river from New Orleans in an area that today is informally known as McDonoghville. Freetown was a section of his land where freed blacks learned to live in independent households awaiting repatriation to Africa. In 1842 alone McDonogh personally oversaw the shipment of eighty of his former slaves to Liberia. The total number of planters who participated in this program and the number of ex-slaves shipped is not certain; with the advent of the Civil War and emancipation of all people of color, the society disbanded. [11]

McDonogh also had close business and social contacts with the free people of color in New Orleans. Although he never married and claimed in his will to have no children, there is speculation that he fathered several children of color. A case in point is Andrew Durnford, the son of Englishman and McDonogh confidant Thomas Durnford (1762-1826) and Rosaline Mercier, free woman of color. McDonogh was the godfather of their first born son Andrew in 1800 and became his mentor and patron, and also was godfather to Andrew's first born son, Thomas McDonogh Durnford in 1826. McDonogh sent him to Lafayette College to study medicine along with several ex-slaves. When Andrew Durnford was asked in court during his father's estate settlement whether Thomas Durnford was his father, the younger Durnford replied, "I answer that I know nothing. The world said there was relationship between the late Thomas Durnford and Myself. There may have been for all I know. It requires a wise man to say who is his father." David Whitten has written a book based on the extensive correspondence between Andrew Durnford from his plantation St. Rosalie in Plaquemines Parish and John McDonogh, titled *Andrew Durnford: A Black Sugar Planter in Antebellum Louisiana.*

The Word Creole: Many Meanings

The creole influence, that centuries-old colonial lifestyle cultivated by the French and Spanish in the West Indies and Louisiana, had to eventually give way to a more cosmopolitan and American world view. The white Creoles were threatened by the massive influx of American businessmen flooding into the city during the early 1800s, and they saw the end of their control over a separate part of New Orleans in 1852, when all municipalities were united under one city government. Although some die-hards spoke only French, shopped only at stores where clerks spoke French, and attended balls and social functions only among other Creoles well into the 1910s, the majority had to make their way in a quickly changing, English speaking world. The antebellum years, so opulent for Americans, were in many ways the twilight years for the Creoles and with them free people of color, who also considered themselves as Creoles.

The term creole is a linguistic anomaly whose true meaning continues to be debated today. Most scholars agree that it comes from the Spanish or Portuguese *criollo or crioulo* meaning created in America, in the New World, as opposed to being created or born in Europe. Joseph G. Tregle, who studied the history of the word creole for decades, concludes that in the French colonies during the seventeenth and eighteenth centuries creole meant simply native-born without reference to color, and that it was used this way in colonial Louisiana as well.

Arnold Bertonneau, activist and Captain in the Union's Louisiana Native Guards (colored). See also page 87. Photo courtesy of his granddaughter Julie Hilla.

References to creole horses, creole architecture, and anything else belonging to the Creoles, including creole slaves, are found throughout colonial writings. [12]

Under the English speaking Americans after the Louisiana Purchase in 1803, a distinction began to emerge among travel writers between Creoles as whites and free people of color as blacks, although among themselves both whites and blacks, even slaves, saw themselves as native born Creoles versus American whites, free blacks and slaves from states like Virginia, the Carolinas, and Mississippi. The term *anci-*

enne population or "old population" was used by white Creoles to refer to the days when they had ruled Louisiana. After the Civil War, when all people where technically free, the term "Creoles of color", appeared to cover non-whites who shared a common history and culture with those of French and Spanish colonial background. In the 1880s New Orleans native George Washington Cable, white and of British descent, wrote a series of short stories about the Creoles of Louisiana from the early 1800s in which he satirized some of the stuffy customs of the whites and glamorized the roles of the free blacks. Immensely popular in the North, his writings were banned by the white Creoles, and Cable eventually left Louisiana. See the bibliography for titles of his work. [13]

History books today continue to use the term Creole to mean ruling class whites, but few people from this group in New Orleans refer to themselves by that term today. Coincidentally, descendants of the Creoles of color have shortened that term to simply Creoles, and *they do*, in some cases, still use it to define who they are. Creole is also a language that was spoken in the French colonies, and a type of which is still used today in Haiti. A different type of Creole was spoken by slaves, free blacks and whites who grew up in close proximity in Louisiana, although children of all classes were encouraged to use French as well. Only a few elderly Louisianians can speak Creole now, but writers like Sybil Kein and her musician brother Deacon John are working in the language in an effort to preserve it. [14]

Due to complex linguistic history, words like "creole cuisine" and "creole cottage" in New Orleans today mean having roots in both white and black Louisiana. Creole cooking, for example, is the type of seasoning and ingredients used for generations by people whose family trees extend back in the state into the 1800s. A creole cottage is a type of simple, small, pitched-roof house developed for both white and black working class people in the old part of the city. With the exportation of jazz music in the 1920s, many of whose practitioners were Creole and of African descent, the term creole became associated with blacks in all-black bands like the Creole Harmonizers. King Oliver's Creole Jazz Band and the Creole Serenaders.

Creole should not be confused with Cajun, the people, along with their customs, food and language, who were expelled by the British from Acadia, a French province in Nova Scotia, Canada in the 1770s. Many of them wandered southward, eventually settling along the swampy bayous of southern Louisiana. A primarily rural population until the 1900s, the Acadians - shortened to Cajuns— have only in recent years been discovered by the rest of the U.S. and brought their spicy food, quaint accent and lively fiddle and accordion music to New Orleans. Like other groups long in Louisiana, some Cajuns have mixed through generations with Indians, Africans and white Creoles; with this mixture has come a blurring of cultural and racial lines, but locals still clearly distinguish between what is Creole and what is Cajun. [15]

The Civil War and
Reconstruction 1860-1890

1860	Dawn of the Civil War. Free people of color owned $15 million in property in N.O., fought on both sides of the war
1862-64	Occupation of N.O. by Union troops
1862-64	*L'Union* French black newspaper published
1863	Emancipation Proclamation issued by A. Lincoln Jan. 1. Grandly celebrated in Congo Square
1863	Corps d'Afrique, 26 regiments of blacks, fight with Union in crucial battle at Port Hudson, Louisiana
1864	Free blacks meet with President A. Lincoln to petition for voting rights, president denies them
1864-68	*La Tribune* replaces *L'Union* as radical black newspaper
1865-69	Freedmen's Bureau regulates labor of blacks in South
1866	July 30: Mechanics Hall Massacre in New Orleans Suffrage convention, many blacks die for right to vote

1867-76	Reconstruction: federal troops enforce the law
1868	Blacks riot over voter registration laws, several die
1868	Louisiana gives blacks citizenship, State constitutional convention passes desegregation laws
1870	Louisiana gives blacks right to vote
1874	Battle of Liberty Place pits Republicans vs White League, some blacks killed
1873-75	Citizens' Committee files suits to enforce Civil Rights laws
1890	Jim Crow (segregation) laws passed by state

The Civil War and
Reconstruction 1860-1890

In 1860 when Abraham Lincoln was elected U.S. President and there was heated talk of Louisiana seceding from the U.S., the free people of color numbered 18,000 in the state and in New Orleans alone they owned $15 million in property. Well experienced as soldiers and proud of their military history, their loyalties would be split, even more than those of the whites, in the bitter Civil War that was to follow. On the one hand, the talk about all slaves being set free jeopardized the plantations and estates of many free people of color who owned and depended on slaves, and also it threatened their privileged status as a separate socio-economic group. Many were intimidated and forced by white associates to enlist as Confederates. On the other hand, their own future was closely aligned with that of all persons of African descent; most experienced ever increasing discrimination by whites, they had family members who were slaves and understood that something had to change. Although they were not officially conscripted to defend either side, they had as much at stake as white southerners did.

How many free men of color fought with the Confederacy in the Civil War to preserve the established order is not certain; some historians put it at approximately 3,000, the majority of whom had been free for generations and came from New Orleans and vicinity. Some of them also lent money to the Confederate government; for example, Bernard Soulie was reported to have extended $10,000 in personal credit. However, more than 20,000 blacks, including many from Louisiana, volunteered to fight with the Union for a new order. During the Battle of Port Hudson north of Baton Rouge in 1863, The Corps d'Afrique, consisting of twenty-six regiments and well over 10,000 black men slave and free, fought valiantly for months under General Nathaniel Banks in a decisive battle of the Civil War. Many blacks died there, including Captain Andre Cailloux in whose honor flags in New Orleans flew half mast for thirty days following his burial. [1]

Some blacks were arrested by Union troops and forced into military service, while many were eager to volunteer. Well trained officers like H. Louis Rey, C.C. Antoine and Francis E. Dumas, wealthy free men of color, distinguished themselves as military leaders of the Louisiana Native Guards, thus allaying the fears of whites that black recruits would prove to be cowards and turncoats. By the end of the war in 1864, black soldiers had won even the praise of President Lincoln for their valor and skill. The Corps d'Afrique disbanded in 1864; its remnants became the Ninth Cavalry and 25th Infantry of the U.S. Army and opened the way for black men to take part in the first and second world wars. [2]

There was a third group of free men of color who did not join either side. Some were needed by their families and businesses and chose to remain civilians, while others fled the city and state with their families in search of peace and prosperity far from the fray. As in the past migrations out of New Orleans, people who had relatives and investments in France, Mexico, Haiti or other countries used these advantages to leave and begin life anew elsewhere. A number of those who stayed

Real estate kingpin and philanthropist Thomy Lafon (1810-1890), a free man of color, donated land and funds to build this asylum at 1125 N. Tonti Street. The asylum moved to Chef Menteur Highway and is now called the Lafon Home.

in the city profited from real estate deals and business contracts during the war. They also formed a political base that would be crucial to the civil rights struggle after the war.

Activism During Occupation

New Orleans fell to Commodore David Farragut and his Federal troops on April 25, 1862 and was occupied for the subsequent two years. During that period, free people of color published their own newspaper *L'Union* which appeared three times weekly and called for civil rights, including suffrage, for educated free blacks. *L'Union* was founded by brothers Louis-

Charles and Jean-Baptiste Roudanez. Louis-Charles Roudanez, the main force behind the paper, was born in New Orleans of French merchant Louis Roudanez and free woman of color Aimée Potens. Educated as a physician in France, he graduated in 1853 and returned to the U.S. to take a second medical degree at Dartmouth College in 1857. By the time of the Civil War he had established a successful medical practice in New Orleans among whites and blacks and had married local woman of color, Celie Saulay. [3]

Roudanez was caught up in a dilemma faced by his community in New Orleans at the time. Many illiterate slaves were being freed or escaping to New Orleans from the countryside in the chaos of the war; in 1865 alone 20,000 arrived in the city. They demanded the same privileges as the long time free people of color but had nothing in common with them. Roudanez in *L'Union* represented his own class, calling for the right for propertied men of color to vote. While he supported the abolition of all slavery, he saw the Freedmen, as the newly freed slaves were called, as a group apart from himself who needed separate help and consideration from the federal government. This attitude was resented by the Freedmen, few of whom could read English, let alone French. It continued to play a role in Louisiana politics for years to come.

January 1, 1863 President Lincoln's Emancipation Proclamation freeing all slaves was celebrated jubilantly in Congo Square in New Orleans. But it would be more than two years until the state legislature adopted the 13th Amendment abolishing all slavery and even longer before masters throughout the state were forced to comply. In late 1863 a black branch of the Union Radical Association was formed in New Orleans calling for a voice in the new civil government that would rule after occupation ended. They were especially outraged that white men who had fought for slavery and the Confederacy in the war were allowed to vote, while educated and propertied men of color who had fought on the winning Union side were not. Their first move was to petition authorities for the right to participate as delegates in the state constitutional convention and to vote for men who would represent them in the state and national legislatures. [4]

The group visited Major George Shepley, Military Governor of Louisiana, and upon getting no assurances from him met with President Lincoln in Washington in March 1864. Led by Jean-Baptiste Roudanez and Arnold Bertonneau from New Orleans, they argued that Louisiana blacks born free before the war and having property and education should be recognized as equals to white men. Lincoln, realizing the influence of the group, was cordial to them, but he offered only to plead their case with state leaders. The next month the state constitutional convention, without black participation, did pass an emancipation law to appease the Radicals but refused to accept the right of black men to vote on state issues.

As the war ended and the soldiers returned home, membership in the Union Radical Association boomed. *L'Union* which had been struggling with financial and ideological problems was replaced with *La Tribune de la Nouvelle Orléans*, which despite its French name was much more inclusive of non-Creole blacks. The first black daily newspaper in the U.S., *La Tribune* included columns in English and had a special weekly edition for rural distribution. Louis Charles Roudanez was still the publisher, but he had joined with Jean-Charles Houzeau, a white radical from Belgium, and the focus of the paper was now to unite all classes of blacks and work together for civil rights. *The Tribune* became so influential that for a time it represented the voice of southern blacks as an official publication read by the U.S. Congress. White planters and intellectuals also paid close attention to its editorials. The newspaper continued until 1870, and although other black newspapers appeared during the late 1800s, including *The Crusader* by lawyer Louis Martinet, none ever enjoyed the same level of success. Today the black monthly *New Orleans Tribune*, published by a descendant of free people of color, is named in its honor. [5]

Effects of the Civil War

After the Civil War and the abolition of slavery, the term free people of color no longer applied, since technically everyone was free. The northern press began to refer to them as Creoles of color. But the differences in identity (Creole vs American), economic class, education and skin tones that had previously existed between various groups of blacks did not suddenly melt away. The heartier families among the former free people of color salvaged their homes and stayed together in their own neighborhoods. The area where the majority of them lived was the Seventh Ward, which includes a number of blocks on both sides of Claiborne Avenue from Esplanade Avenue to St. Bernard Avenue. In 1865 they may not have had much food in the house, but they still had their family honor, and on Sundays they continued to dress in fine clothes and attend mass. They intermarried, kept their Creole language and traditions and often refused to send their children to schools with other blacks.

Free black planters and farmers had their properties burned by Union troops just like whites did. Real estate values plummeted, credit was hard to come by, and landowners were forced to pay outrageous taxes. Depression and suicide claimed some lives, while others were forced into poverty and menial jobs. A few lucky ones, like Thomy Lafon, Aristide Mary, Oscar Dunn and Edmund Dupuy, profited from the low real estate market, but most people had to eke out a living, the same as their white neighbors.

But not everything was bleak; 1865 was a watershed year with the Civil War ending that spring. Louise DeMortie, famous northern black poet, was well received in a series of readings she gave in New Orleans, and the symphonic pieces of native son, black composer Edmund Dédé, were featured in a concert at Orleans Theater. In January the Convention of Colored Men with delegates from around the state met in New Orleans. The 102 men in attendance drew up a basic platform for political action. Soon they would join with the Equal Rights League, a national organization which later became the Universal Suffrage Association. After the assassination of President Lincoln in April, the USA held its convention in New Orleans in September as the new Republican Party. Despite being legally disenfranchised, the votes of blacks of all classes helped send Henry Clay Warmoth (white) to represent them in Washington. [6]

There was also the problem of the Freedmen, most of them poor American blacks who flocked to New Orleans for jobs and opportunities after the war, where they were met with a series of rules similar to the restrictions that had been imposed before the war on free people of color. This alienated them from the Creoles of color, but illiterate and politically naive, the Freedmen depended on the education and political expertise and connections of the French speaking blacks to represent them in the new and rapidly changing world of Reconstruction. The Freedmen's Bureau that operated from 1865-1869, established by the U.S. Congress to regulate the labor situation for newly freed blacks, was assisted by the free men of color and the New Orleans Freedmen's Aid Association which tried to form co-ops of black workers to borrow money and rent or lease abandoned plantations. Unfortunately, this effort met with only temporary and limited success.

The Mechanics Hall Massacre

Nowhere in the post-Civil War South was the political leadership of blacks as effective as in New Orleans. The heroic measures of local black men in a bloody confrontation with police on July 30, 1866 had a profound effect on the U.S. Congress, bringing about swift passage of the 15th Amendment which gave all men – regardless of race – the right to vote. [7] The Friends of Universal Suffrage were meeting in the city in the hall of the Mechanics' Institute located where the Roosevelt Hotel now stands. Attended by prominent men of both races, the meeting July 27 had ended in heated debates on the vote for some free men but not others. A second meeting for July 30 was scheduled. Five thousand torch bearing blacks demonstrated meanwhile at the Henry Clay statue nearby, evoking the spirit of John Brown and other antislavery heroes. The city called in a special police force made up of ex-Confederates to handle anticipated crowds. On July 30 thousands of blacks, joined by some white sympathizers, converged on the Mechanics' Institute from various directions of the city; skirmishes broke out between them and the police all along Canal Street.

The police and demonstrators exchanged fire in the crowd, causing panic. At the convention pandemonium reigned when police stormed the building and shot point blank at men huddled in corners of the hall, their hands in the air waving white handkerchiefs. The police charged four separate times, each time seeking out black leaders to beat, stab and shoot. The

Scene from the Mechanics Hall Massacre in New Orleans as portrayed in Harper's Weekly September 8, 1866. Photo courtesy of Amistad Research Center.

melee was finally under control by late afternoon and martial law was imposed. A total of 214 people were killed or wounded and hundreds arrested; the dead included one policeman, two white delegates to the meeting, and 35 blacks. Dr. A. P. Dostie, a dentist and black radical leader, was among the dead. In the days following the event, houses were searched at random, arms confiscated and more blacks arrested. The event variously described in the black press as the Mechanics Hall Massacre and in the white press as the New Orleans Riot or the Riot of 1866, was investigated by a select congressional committee which put the blame on both the black demonstrators and the white police. [8]

Within a year, pressured by the Mechanics Hall incident and similar riots in Memphis about the same time, Congress passed the Military Reconstruction Acts which included the right of blacks to vote. The *Comité des Citoyens* or Citizens' Committee formed immediately in New Orleans by Creole and American blacks to register newly enfranchised voters and unite black leadership. In no time 82,907 registered black voters seriously outnumbered white voters in Louisiana. Reconstruction, as the 1867 Acts were called, imposed federal military control over the ex-Confederate states, a move never accepted by whites as legitimate. But it gave blacks an opportunity for the first time to participate in state and national government.

A contingent of 98 delegates, half of them black, dubbed the White and Tan Convention, drew up the new state constitution of 1868 which included civil rights clauses and a call for integrated public schools. Though few whites voted for the new constitution, it was approved by a majority of the states' voters, who also elected Henry Clay Warmoth (white) as governor and Oscar J. Dunn (black) as lieutenant governor. Dunn died suddenly – it was rumored that he was poisoned, and Warmoth was impeached in 1872. This gave an American black, P.B.S. Pinchback, a brief stint as governor, the highest political office held by a black in the United States up to that time. [9]

Despite the appearance of political progress for blacks, locally imposed strict voter registration rules soon became a new barrier. In the fall of 1868 another race riot erupted in the streets of New Orleans. It started as a series of minor skirmishes, culminating Saturday, October 24 in a free-for-all fight between opposing political ward marching bands, The Workingmen's Club (Democrat) and a procession of Republican clubs with large contingents of blacks. Looting and random attacks on both sides went on through the night. Casualties vary according to reports, but at least seven whites and thirteen blacks lost their lives, including the ten year old son of state senator C.C. Antoine who was trampled to death. [10]

The Advent of Jim Crow

The Citizens' Committee shunned violence, rather becoming active in the courts by initiating a series of legal cases to enforce the civil rights guaranteed by Congress in the 1870s but often denied locally. Josephine Decuir, an elegant, light skinned Creole woman, was a precursor to Alabama's Rosa Parks of the 1960s when Decuir in 1873 sued the owner of the steamboat *Governor Allen* because she was refused entrance into the ladies' cabin due to her color. In 1875 the Louisiana Supreme Court awarded her $1000, but that decision was reversed in 1877. Two black men sued the St. Charles Theater in 1875 when they were overcharged for drinks that had had salt added. But the landmark case that put Louisiana on the map was *Plessy v Ferguson* when the Committee was rejuvenated in 1890. Homer Plessy, a Creole of color from New Orleans, contested the state's first segregation law requiring separate railroad cars for blacks and whites. Plessy boarded a white car and refused to move. His case went eventually to the U.S. Supreme Court in 1896 but was decided against him. [11]

The court ruled that states had the right to maintain separate but equal public facilities for blacks and for whites. The decision ushered in a spate of Jim Crow laws throughout the South that would not be successfully overturned until the 1960s. Jim Crow, a white performer in blackface in a popular minstrel show of the time, became the symbol of blacks and segregation to radicals fighting racial discrimination. Historically, it stood to reason that funds, legal staffs and volunteers for these various early civil rights cases would come from New Orleans where blacks had for generations been free, received educations and been politically active. Black women there were also involved, supporting the men in their dangerous protests. The Committee of 500 Women, formed in 1876 in New Orleans by Mrs. Mary Garrett (later Nelson), a black woman, fought for equal rights for all and encouraged blacks to migrate to northern states where opportunities depended less on skin color. [12]

White backlash in the form of para-military groups, like the Knights of the White Camellia, formed in 1868, and the White League in 1874, tried to terrorize activist blacks and keep them from voting. The White League is remembered for a confrontation it had in New Orleans September 14, 1874 with Metropolitan Police of which the majority of officers and members were

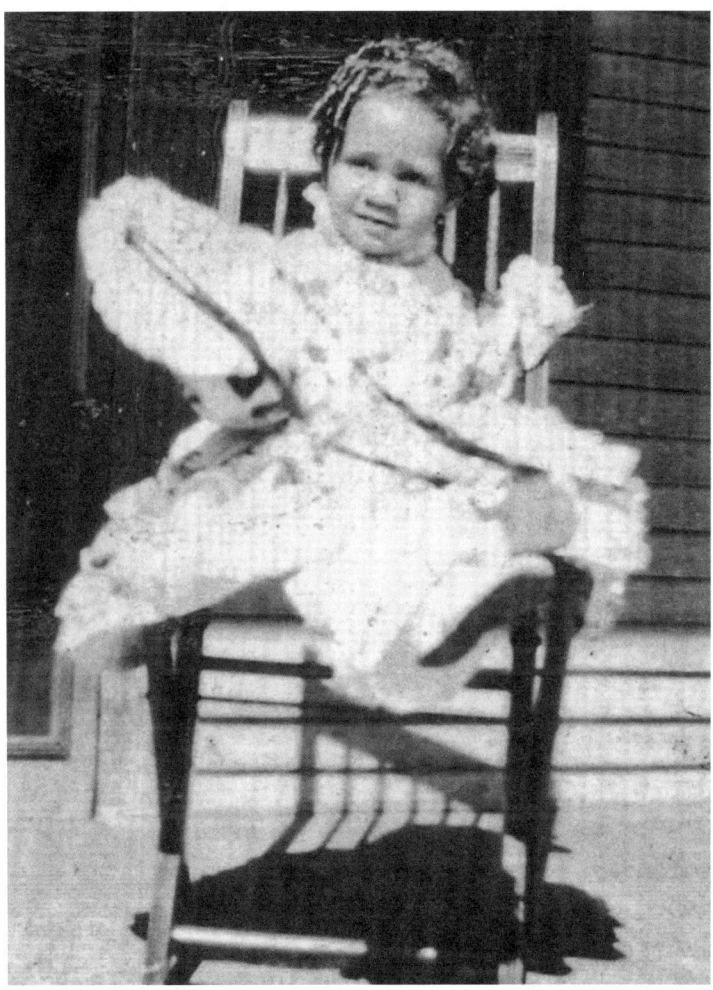

A young Creole child, Dorothy Hunt, poses for a photo at her home in New Orleans ca. 1919. Photo courtesy of her daughter Albertine Norwood.

black. The League demonstrated at the foot of Canal Street for a Democrat governor to replace the Republican in office. When the police tried to arrest them, a fierce fifteen minute battle ensued in which thirty men died, most of them police, including a few blacks. [13]

Claiming victory, the White League erected a monument near the spot to honor their men who had reimposed white supremacy. The black press reported the incident as the Metropolitan Police Riot and the white press as the Battle of Liberty Place. The statue was moved a block away from that site at the foot of Canal Street when Harrah's Casino was built – it stands between the Aquarium of the Americas and the parking lot entrance to Canal Place shopping complex.

The Creole Legacy Continues

1911	Book *Our People and Our History* chronicles free people of color in Louisiana
1917	Xavier University founded in N.O as only Catholic university for blacks in the U.S.
1920s	Jazz develops as a musical form, joins black musicians, Creole and American; many move to northern cities
1935	Straight College and New Orleans University (both for blacks) merge to form Dillard University
1941	New Orleans YWCA provides integrated facility in city for blacks and whites to meet and dialogue
1954	Pontchatrain Park, middle class housing development built. Southern University founded nearby in 1960s as black equivalent of University of New Orleans
1954	Supreme Court rules in Brown v Board of Education that public facilities must be integrated
1957	Southern Christian Leadership Conference formed in New Orleans, launches Civil Rights Era and career of Martin L. King

1958-60	Greater New Orleans Bridge over Mississippi constructed, interstate highway overpass cuts through, destroys traditional Creole of color area
1960s	Court ordered desegregation of public schools in N.O. 1964-68, U.S. Congress passes series of civil rights acts prohibiting all forms of racial discrimination
1970s	New Orleans East is developed as suburban housing, many middle class blacks build or buy houses there
1977	Ernest N. "Dutch" Morial elected first black mayor of New Orleans, blacks active in city politics
1980	Armstrong Park opens, thus revitalizing Congo Square

The Creole Legacy Continues

Today in New Orleans the press and other media use the terms "black" or "African-American" to refer to anyone of African descent. Technically then, there is no more distinction between Creole and American blacks, between people whose families date back to the founding fathers of the city and those whose grandparents or parents migrated there in this century.

But to anyone who observes New Orleans social, political and racial patterns, it is very clear that "Creole" is a term used frequently by blacks among themselves for those who carry on the names, traditions, family businesses and social positions of the free people of color, and as such that they continue to face some of the same issues at the end of the twentieth century that their ancestors did two hundred years ago. Light skin, European features, long straight or wavy black hair and a French surname earn some blacks privilege and status above others among whites, yet they also evoke disgust and anger among darker skinned blacks with English surnames who feel discriminated against by such favored members of their own race. Though rarely discussed in the media or other open forums, this infra-racial situation affects the politics, social order, jobs and businesses of the city in many ways.

Conflict and Confusion

Colored Creole; Color Conflict and Confusion is a booklet by Aline St. Julien published in 1977 to explain the identity crisis she has shared with hundreds of other Creole descendants. Her insular upbringing in a closely knit Seventh Ward community, attendance at the Catholic all-black Xavier Preparatory School and a social life limited primarily to Corpus Christi Catholic Church and the Autocrat Club did not prepare her for the civil rights movement of the 1960s nor the Black is Beautiful campaign. When as a teenager St. Julien let her straightened hair grow out in its natural kinky form and embraced her long repressed African heritage, her family was appalled. She writes of the debilitating self-hate she and others like her have had to overcome in order to acknowledge who they really are and find their places in a world that still sees issues in terms of black or white.

W.E.B. Dubois, the black intellectual who despite his French surname was not from Louisiana, wrote about the paradox of "two-ness" with which he wrestled in the early 1900s, as ambivalence about racial identity felt by people of mixed European and African ancestry. [1] The subject continues to fascinate and pain people today, but in Louisiana it has very real implications, especially in families where some members have crossed the color line as *pass en blanc*, passing for white. As recently as August 16, 1993 the *Times-Picayune*, daily newspaper of New Orleans, carried an article in which Ulysses S. Ricard, a local Creole, explained how his father's obituary on his death in 1975 had not appeared in the paper because four of his father's thirteen siblings "were living as white people and did not want to be listed... as survivors". The obituary was published in the 1993 article but still without the four siblings' names. Ironically, Ricard Jr., researcher and archivist of Creole history and genealogy, also died within months of the article; his loss is widely acknowledged among scholars and historians.

Race Consciousness

Race consciousness has deep roots in a city where one's family name and status are carefully guarded and where until 1970 the state law read that anyone with "any traceable amount" of black bloodlines was defined as black. From 1949 to 1965 Naomi Drake, a white woman heading up the Bureau of Vital Statistics for New Orleans, took it upon herself to withhold documents from thousands of families whose birth or death certificates listed them as white but whom she personally suspected of having black blood. In many cases she changed the race on such documents from white to black. When she was finally fired in 1965 her office showed a backlog of 4,700 requests for birth certificates that had not been filled and another 1,200 for death certificates. [2]

In 1970 state law was changed to read that anyone with "one thirty-second or less of Negro blood" was defined as black. That law was challenged in 1977 when Susie Guillory Phipps made national headlines for suing the state to have her race on her birth certificate changed from black to white. An olive skinned woman with dark hair and eyes, Phipps argued that she had grown up as a white child in Frey Community, a predominantly German and Cajun rural settlement near Iota in southern Louisiana. The first time she saw her birth certificate was in 1977 when she wanted to apply for a passport to travel with her businessman husband Andy Phipps. Discovering in the Bureau of Vital Statistics that the certificate listed her as black, she cancelled the trip and instead pursued a court case to get the document changed.

The case was finally heard in 1980 and settled in 1983

Formal portrait circa 1920s of an unidentified couple from New Orleans. Marriages of light skinned blacks with darker complected blacks were discouraged among Creoles. Photo courtesy of Albertine Norwood.

when the court ruled against Phipps. Evidence was presented at the trial showing that Phipps' family had been considered and treated as black when she was a child, and furthermore that her family tree included Margarita, a slave woman who in the 1770s became the mistress of French planter Gregoire Guillory, giving the 46 year old Phipps three thirty-seconds of black blood. The case went on to the Fourth District Court of Appeals but after losing there and having spent over $40,000, Phipps gave up. Although she was never able to get her birth certificate changed, she stimulated the state legislature to repeal the old law. Today one has to establish "a preponderance of evidence" of race rather than base it on a set formula. Birth certificates, if they list race at all, are to give whatever race the mother stated for her newborn child. [3]

The Creoles and the
Civil Rights Movement

At the turn of the century as segregation laws took hold and all blacks were made to sit at the back of the streetcar and use drinking fountains marked "Colored" regardless of lightness of skin tone, Creole blacks who remained in the downtown areas of Tremé and Faubourg Marigny, called "below Canal Street", were separated from uptown blacks who were generally not of Creole background. Protestants by religion and often unskilled laborers, uptown blacks spoke no French and had little regard for the better educated Creoles. But the two groups were sometimes drawn together by circumstances beyond their control.

The Creole musicians, for example, who had been educated to play classical pieces at symphonies and mostly white gatherings, were forbidden to play for anyone except blacks. When the District, dubbed Storyville, permitting gambling and prostitution opened in 1898 outside the old French part of the city, the brothels, clubs and saloons offered lucrative pay to musicians. Soon uptown blacks were playing in the same halls as Creole blacks; the Creoles taught the uptowners how to read musical notes, while the free wheeling rhythms and style of the uptowners began to predominate in what would later be known as jazz. Ferdinand LeMenthe (LaMothe), who became famous as ragtime player Jelly Roll Morton, is typical of the Creole blacks who were greatly influenced by the amalgamation of both groups. Louis Armstrong, a contemporary of Morton, is representative of its influence on the uptowners.

When Storyville closed in 1918, it was the Creole musicians who had the contacts and means to sign on to play on the boats headed upriver and establish jazz clubs in St. Louis, Chicago and New York. King Oliver, a Creole from New Orleans, for example, was the mentor of Louis Armstrong and helped to make him famous in northern cities. [4]

In politics too, downtown Creoles and uptowners found that cooperation was essential in beating the specter of separate-but-equal facilities. Because of its Creole history. New Orleans blacks and whites shared an intimacy that transcended race and was not found in other parts of the country. This made surreptitious meetings between the races possible in private homes or the YWCA, one of the only integrated public spots in the 1950s. It also helped prevent race riots and brought about a relatively peaceful integration of the streetcars, buses and schools in the

1960s. Support from liberal wealthy whites to black institutions such as Flint-Goodrich Hospital and Nursing School, Xavier and Dillard universities and Pontchartrain Park Housing Development were facilitated through the trust and confidence of people of both races.

This aspect attracted Martin Luther King who had close personal ties to New Orleans, visited the city often and helped found the Southern Christian Leadership Conference at the New Zion Baptist Church in central New Orleans in 1957 because of the extensive network and support system of blacks and whites in that city. The Conference, along with the extensive history of black resistance and activism in New Orleans, launched the civil rights era with King as its most famous leader. One wonders today what different turn history may have taken had King accepted a position of chaplain at Dillard University in New Orleans, offered to him in 1955, rather than returned that year to the bus boycott in Montgomery, Alabama. [5]

What Makes a Person a Creole?

The faces of black people in New Orleans today offer a wide ranging palette of racial characteristics that include everything from the darkest hues of ebony skin to the high cheekbones of the American Indian and green eyes of the European. The problem of defining people by sight as to their race was exemplified in 1992 when several light skinned blacks in New Orleans finally challenged a decade-long practice by many grocery stores and check cashing outlets of writing code words on the backs of personal checks as to the race of the customer. Such identification was supposed to help in investigating stolen or kited checks. After being asked repeatedly and point blank by cashiers whether they were black or white, while other customers were not subjected to such prying, the disgruntled light skinned blacks protested in a November 13,1992 *Times-Picayune* article. "If they have to ask my race," said one complainant, "what good can it be to them?"

What then makes a person Creole today? It's not the neighborhood, because since the early 1960s the construction of a massive Interstate 610 overpass has decimated Claiborne Avenue and the Seventh Ward, causing businesses and families to move into the more suburban areas of Gentilly and New Orleans East. Claiborne Avenue was once a peaceful oak lined

The Autocrat Club on St. Bernard Avenue was the club for Creole social life in the early to mid-1900s. Today many of its members no longer live in the immediate vicinity.

boulevard similar to what fashionable St. Charles Avenue is today uptown, and a center of Creole economic and social life. Today only a few of the shops and businesses are surviving there in what has become one of the most crime-ridden areas in the city. [6]

Creole can best be defined today as a state of mind and of heritage. It means being Catholic, a parishioner of Corpus Christi, St. Augustine or St. Leo the Great churches and sending one's children to parochial schools like St. Mary's, Xavier Prep or St. Aug. It means membership in one of the social clubs like the Autocrat or the Original Illinois. Family comes first with close attention paid to observing birthdays, baptisms and First Communions; holidays are invariably spent together. Most Creole children have a *marraine* and/or *parraine*, godmother and godfather, who take their roles seriously. It means having heard basic French or Creole phrases as a child and peppering one's speech with terms like *compere* or *commere*, meaning close friend, *galerie* for porch or balcony, *banquette* for sidewalk and *tisane* for a medicinal tea. It means cooking a great gumbo, making groceries (going to the supermarket) or going to the quarters (visiting the French Quarter) and referring to two o'clock in the afternoon as "evening". These are creolisms that have been adapted by the larger community in New Orleans as well, and Creole traditions such as visiting the cemetery on All Saints Day, eating king cake during the Carnival season and presenting one's teenage daughter to society at a debutante party are practiced by both whites and blacks who cannot claim a drop of Creole blood.[7]

Whether or not Creole is a race in itself or a separate

identity that should be recognized by census takers and sociologists is argued from time to time. Gilbert E. Martin, Sr. of New Orleans calls for a "Creole nationhood" in his book *Creoles: A Shattered Nation* published in 1981. "I contend," he writes," that Creoles are a unique race of people... [with] specific traits and traditions that have been transmitted from generation to generation by Creole speaking people, a unique nation of mixed-bloods."

Overlooked in Mainstream History Books

Creoles of color and their ancestors, the free people of color, have tended to be overlooked and ignored by mainstream historians despite information written and published by them. An elderly Rodolphe Desdunes, whose parents had migrated

Ernest N. "Dutch" Morial celebrates his election as the first black mayor of New Orleans as his children and wife look on. He served two four-year terms 1978-1986. His son Marc (not pictured here) was elected N.O. Mayor in 1994.

from St. Domingue (Haiti), published a book in French in 1921 about the free people of color he had known and who had contributed to the community in New Orleans, *Nos Hommes et Notre Histoire* (Our People and Our History). Published in Canada, and selective about the individuals it profiled, Desdunes' book had a small circulation limited to mostly French speaking families in Louisiana. Finally in 1973, an English translation was made available. Alice Moore Dunbar Nelson, New Orleans author, wrote a substantial article "People of Color in Louisiana" which appeared in the 1916-17 edition of T*he Journal of Negro History*. And in 1937 Charles B. Rousseve, local historian of color, came out with his book *The Negro in Louisiana: Aspects of His History and His Literatur*e. In 1945 *Gumbo Ya-Ya*, a collection of Louisiana folktales gathered by the Works Progress Administration (WPA) Louisiana Writers' Project, featured the collaboration of Marcus B. Christian, Supervisor of the Negro Writers' Project. A 1200 page manuscript by Christian, "The Negro in Louisiana", has never been published.

The 1990s may be a decade when this oversight among historians is corrected. In 1993 alone two major books, *Creole New Orleans* (Hirsch & Logsdon) and *Africans in Colonial Louisiana* (Hall), were published by Louisiana State University Press. In 2000 the same press brought out the landmark volume *Creole: The History and Legacy of Louisiana's Free People of Color*, a collection of scholarly essays edited by Dr. Sybil Kein. The Louisiana State Museum in its permanent exhibit in the Cabildo in New Orleans, newly reopened in 1994, portrays the role of free people of color in the city where such people lived and worked.

Another important work in 1993 in interpreting this aspect of history is *The Myth of New Orleans in Literature: Dialogues of Race and Gender* by Violet Harrington Bryan. In American literature free people of color have appeared now and then in fiction as peripheral and racially ambiguous characters. The exception is the quadroon, the beautiful mulatto woman whom the dashing young white man loves but can never marry, a haunting and tragic figure whose fate is sealed by her African-tainted blood. She is a major character in the novels (see the bibliography at the back of this book for authors and publishers): *The Quadroone or St. Michael's Day*, (1841), *The Octoroon in Paris* (1849) *The Quadroon* (1856) *Old Creole Days* (1879), *The Grandissimes* (1880) *Madame Delphine* (1881), *Towards the Gulf: A Romance of Louisian*a (1887), *Monsieur Mott* (1888), *A Mystery of New Orleans* (1890), *Les Quarteronnes de la Nouvelle Orléan*s (1894), T*oucoutou*(1928), *Absalom! Absalom*! (1936), *Rampart Stree*t (1948), and *The Feast of All Saints* (1979).

Many descendants of the free people of color today are unaware of their personal history and the events that formed it. Their parents and grandparents in some cases simply did not talk openly about the family background. Sometimes it was too painful and complicated to explain fortunes that had been lost or relatives who passed for white and did not want to be associated with black-identified siblings or cousins. The author has interviewed a number of people who identify as Creoles and descendants of free people of color in New Orleans; many told of childhoods in which little was said about family trees and ancestors, or where white people attended black funerals or visited in Creole homes disguised as friends, when in fact they were blood relatives.

One woman mentioned a portrait of a white man that hung in the house of her grandmother where she grew up. No one ever asked who the man was, though he was obviously not George Washington or Abraham Lincoln. The portrait has been lost and there is no one left to identify it. If the free people of color wrote diaries and letters in the early years and during antebellum New Orleans, no such mementos have surfaced in local archives. One Creole, whose grandmother was a vaudeville performer in the 1920s, spoke of a family tree "with many bent branches". Given the racially polarized climate in the 20th century, artifacts that white families might have had of black relatives and vice versa have probably been lost or purposely destroyed.

Exporting the Creole Lifestyle

When one considers the talents and skills of thousands upon thousands of free people of color and their descendants who have left New Orleans and Louisiana through the centuries, seeking acceptance and equality in other countries and other parts of the U.S., the figure is staggering. It is a brain drain of enormous proportion, measured in part by the success that such people have met elsewhere in almost every possible profession.

Although there appear to be few ongoing connections between Creoles in New Orleans and countries where they migrated in large numbers in the eighteenth and nineteenth centuries, such as Haiti, Cuba, Mexico and France, Creole com-

Claiborne Avenue, a tranquil, elegant, oak-lined boulevard in the heart of the Creole community (above) was replaced in the early 1960s by an overpass to the Interstate 10 highway system (below).

munities exist in several parts of the United States. The largest outside New Orleans is in Los Angeles where dozens of families migrated, first in the late 1930s and early 1940s because of wartime industries that were hiring workers there, and in the late 1940s and early 1950s as blacks sought refuge from segregation in Louisiana.

The Sunset Limited, a train that still runs the 2,000 miles between New Orleans and Los Angeles, became a line of communication for many years. Creoles working on the train would describe the "promised land" of southern California to friends and family in New Orleans, and news from both cities was transmitted by train workers. In the 1950s there was even a stretch of Jefferson Boulevard in Los Angeles called Little New Orleans with the St. Bernard Market, Merlin Saulny's Restaurant, Duplantier's Barber Shop, and the Big Loaf Bakery, the only place in Los Angeles that made New Orleans style French bread. Today families with means have moved farther out into the suburbs, and the Creole community there is more diverse. However, family ties remain strong, efforts are made to socialize with people of like heritage throughout the year, and an annual reunion of Creoles brings together people from throughout the southern part of the state.[8] Rebie Turnage's novel *Louisiana Love* (1984) is a nostalgic account by a woman from that community about her childhood memories of growing up Creole in her home state of Louisiana.

Pockets of New Orleans based Creole families can be found in other parts of California and the country at large. In the early 1900s northern cities like Chicago, St. Louis and New York became home to many Creole musicians. Hundreds of black workers moved north for factory jobs. As with the migration to California, trains provided transportation, jobs and an ongoing communication system with these cities and New Orleans. Steamboats and later cargo ships also lured many workers into jobs that took them north on a regular basis. Most of these families are today well assimilated into African-American communities in these various cities.

In recent years there have been signs of a modest reverse migration with children and grandchildren of Creoles who left New Orleans over half a century ago coming back to visit relatives and discover the places so often talked about in their childhood. Some of these visitors feel a comfort and acceptance they have not experienced in their own cities; when job and business opportunities are available, the temptation to stay is enhanced.

The future of the descendants of the free people of color as a distinct group is uncertain. The challenge is to preserve their unique cultural heritage in a way that it continues to have meaning to younger Creoles. Today, more so than ever, they run the risk of being called separatists and snobs if they speak French and emphasize their history and contributions. Conversely, when they relinquish their ties to the past in order to merge into the larger African-American population, a delicate piece of the American experience is forever lost.

End Notes

Note: to conserve space, all publications and manuscripts referred to here are listed with full title, author, publisher and date in the Bibliography and Suggested Reading section. The author's name follows title in parentheses here.

Chapter 1:
Founding and Early Years 1718-1730

1. For detailed statistics on this topic see chapter 3 of *Africans in Colonial Louisiana* (Hall). See also "From African Captivity to American Slavery: The Introduction of Black Laborers to Louisiana" (Usner).

2. "Free Persons of Color in Colonial Louisiana" (Everett) explains the role of Africans as slaves and later free people, giving a number of examples from the 1720s and 1730s.

3. Lives of early free blacks are detailed in "Black New Orleans 1718-1938" (Christian).

4. A full interpretation and explanation of the Black Code is given in "Slave Policies in French Louisiana" (Allain).

5. For information on the Natchez Massacre and its impact see *Africans in Colonial Louisiana* (Hall) pp. 99-112.

Chapter 2:
The French Period 1773-1762

1. "The Negro in Louisiana" (Christian) chapter 21 mentions the use of many slaves by the Ursulines and their kindness to them. "Free Persons of Color in Louisiana" (Everett) p. 45-46 tells of two cases of Capuchins freeing their slaves.

2. For transcription of these cases see The Louisiana Historical Quarterly volume 19 of 1936: Baraca - p. 471-478, Marie Jeanne - p. 1112-1116.

3. Examples and names of slaves winning or buying their freedom are found in "Free Persons of Color in Colonial Louisiana" (Everett). See also "Avenues to Freedom Open to New Orleans' Black Population, 1769-1779" (Hanger).

4. For a complete history of this market and Congo Square, see "New Orleans's Congo Square: An Urban setting for Early Afro-American Culture Formation" (Johnson).

Chapter 3:
The Spanish Period 1763-1802

1. "The Negro in Louisiana" (Christian) chapter 21 tells of Markandal and other influences of St. Domingue slaves on those in New Orleans.

2. Kimberly Hanger has done extensive research and writing on blacks during the Spanish Period. For freeing of slaves see her article "Avenues to Freedom Open to New Orleans' Black Population 1769-1779."

3. Fiehrer's essay is published in the book *Louisiana's Black Heritage* p. 3-31.

4. Hanger's article "Household and Community Structure Among the Free Population of Spanish New Orleans, 1778" gives detailed census material for that year, including sex ratios, sizes of households, and family types for both blacks and whites.

5. Hanger names and discusses cases of slave women freed on the basis of sexual liaisons in "Avenues to Freedom Open to New Orleans' Black Population 1769-1779" p. 249. "Racial openness" is also discussed in *Africans in Colonial Louisiana* (Hall) p. 240-241. The article " 'Open and Notorious' Concubinage: The Emancipation of Slave Mistresses by Will and the Supreme Court in Antebellum Louisiana" (Schafer) explains how the practice flourished in the pre-Civil Wars years.

6. See above references for more information on plaçage. "The Vieux Carre Survey", which traces property histories of buildings in the French Quarter, documents free women of color property owners of the Spanish and early American periods. State supreme court records at the library of the University of New Orleans Public Library show how such property was often acquired.

7. The case of Vidal is mentioned by de Laussat in his *Memoirs of My Life* p. 102 and in succession records. The Metoyer history is given in *The Forgotten People: Cane River's Creoles of Color* (Mills).

8. These theories on naming patterns are derived by the author from studies of many colonial records and documents and from conversations with Creoles.

9. *Africans in Colonial Louisiana* (Hall) deals in various sections with runaway slaves. For more information see "Cimarrones and the San Malo Band in Spanish Louisiana" (Din).

10. The 1785-86 laws are discussed in "Free Persons of Color in Louisiana" (Everett) p. 34.

11. This period and the Pointe Coupée Uprising are covered in "Cimarrones and the San Malo Band" (Din), in "Conflicting Loyalties: The French Revolution and Free People of Color in Spanish New Orleans" (Hanger), in "The Abortive Slave Revolt at Pointe Coupée, Louisiana, 1795" (Holmes), and in *Africans in Colonial Louisiana* (Hall) chapter 8.

Chapter 4:
Louisiana Purchase and Early American Years 1803-1830

1. Chapters 4 and 5 of *Creole New Orleans* (Hirsch) discuss in detail the transition from Creole to American government. "The Vieux Carre Survey" indicates which properties were owned by free blacks in 1803.

2. This period is described from personal experience by C.C. Robin in *Voyage to Louisiana* 1803-1805. For more information see *Creole New Orleans* (Hirsch) and "The Free People of Color in New Orleans 1803-1860" (McGowan) and "The Negro in Louisiana" (Christian).

3. A detailed account of a Louisiana revolt is the book *On to New Orleans! Louisiana's Historic 1811 Slave Revolt* by Albert Thrasher (1995), privately published. Contact Cypress Press, 2440 Chartres Street, New Orleans, LA 70117.

4. For research on this and subsequent migrations to Mexico, see the article "The Louisiana Creole – Mexico Connection" by Mary Gehman.

5. Names and family histories of a number of free blacks who settled these suburbs are given in two volumes of The New Orleans Architecture Series, one titled *Faubourg-Tremé* and the Bayou Road, and the other volume *Faubourg- Marigny*. The latter has photographs of many of the buildings they constructed and occupied.

6. For more information on slave revolts of the time see 'En Garde': The Effects of Slave Insurrection upon the Louisiana Mentality 1811-1815" (Rodriguez). See also chapter 5 of *Creole New Orleans* (Hirsch).

7. City directories of the period, available in most local archives, list hundreds of people noted as fmc or fwc (free man or woman of color) and their occupations or businesses. See also "The Negro in Louisiana" (Christian) and "The Forgotten People: Free People of Color in New Orleans 1850-1879" (Rankin), part 3.

8. For an overview of voodoo, its roots in Creole Louisiana, and its practice in New Orleans, see "Beware of Premature Autopsies: Hoodoo in New Orleans Literature" (Senter).

9. For information on blacks who fought in the Battle of New Orleans, see *Negro Soldiers in the Battle of New Orleans* (Christian) and *Negro Soldiers- Free Men of Color in the Battle of New Orleans War of 1822* (Loomis).

10. Most writers on the free people of color mention the Quadroon balls. Comprehensive references are "Quadroon Balls in the Spanish Period" (Morazan) and "The Quadroons" (Gayarre).

11. Locations of quadroon balls are discussed in detail in "The Negro in Louisiana" (Christian). "The Vieux Carre Survey" also shows such balls as occurring at the Davis Dance Hall.

12. See chapter 7 of this book and *The Myth of New Orleans in Literature* (Bryan).

Chapter 5:
Antebellum years 1830-1860

1. These laws are discussed in "Antebellum Free Persons of Color in Postbellum Louisiana" (Schweninger) and Chapter One of *Black New Orleans* 1860-1880 (Blassingame). Chapter Four of *Creole New Orleans* (Hirsch) covers the period in general.

2. Property sales and reasons for them come from "The Vieux Survey".

3. See more on this period in "The Forgotten People: Free People of Color in New Orleans 1850-1870" (Rankin).

4. Copies of *Les Cenelles* are rare: Amistad Research Center and the Historic New Orleans Collection both have a copy locally. Some of the poems with English translations are included in Alfred J. Guillaume's essay "Love, Death and Faith in the New Orleans Poets of Color" published in the book *In Old New Orleans* (Holditch).

5. "The Negro in Louisiana" (Christian) has several chapters on political developments in antebellum and post Civil War Louisiana. See chapter 19 regarding the 1830s and 1840s.

6. Information on businessmen named in this chapter was compiled from city directories, property records and the writings and papers of Marcus Christian housed in the library of the University of New Orleans.

7. The Macarty families (both white and of color) were prominent in Louisiana during this period. *Free Negro Owners of Slaves in the United States in 1830* (Woodson) lists Cecée Macarty as owning 32 slaves and several other Macartys of color as owning from 5 to 8 slaves each.

8. *Our People, Our History* (Desdunes) praises the legacy of Madame Couvent. A more complete reference is *A History of Saint Louis School of Holy Redeemer* (Gallaher).

9. See the history of the Sisters of the Holy Family, *Violets in the King's Garden* written by Sister Mary Borgia and published by the order in 1976. Sister Boniface Adams, current historian of the order, has compiled additional information.

End Notes

10. See *Andrew Durnford: A Black Sugar Planter in Antebellum Louisiana* (Whitten) for an extensive history of McDonogh.

11. Most standard histories of this period discuss the American Colonization Society. For more on McDonogh's participation see "John McDonogh, Slave-Owner" (Kendall).

12. Tregle's essay "Creoles and Americans" in the book *Creole New Orleans* (Hirsch) sums up his theories on the derivation and use of the term "Creole". Another extensive reference is *White by Definition: Social Classification in Creole Louisiana*, in which anthropologist Virginia Dominguez delineates various distinctions of skin color, culture and language.

13. Much has been written about Cable (1844-1925), the Creole controversy, and his relationship to other writers of his time. See the definitive book on his life and work. *George W. Cable: A Biography* (Turner).

14. Kein, professor emeritus of English at the University of Michigan, has published *Gombo People: New Orleans Creole Poetry* in the Creole language. Deacon John, her brother, is a popular New Orleans musician.

15. *The Encyclopedia of Southern Culture* (Wilson) explains the differences between Creoles and Cajuns in language, customs, etc.

Chapter 6:
The Civil War and Reconstruction
1860-1890

1. The role of blacks in the Civil War is detailed in *Black New Orleans* (Blassingame). Flags flying half mast for Cailoux are mentioned in "The Negro in Louisiana" (Christian).

2. For names and numbers of African-Americans who fought in the Civil War see *Who's Who in Colored Louisiana* (Perkins). "The Negro in Louisiana" (Christian) chapter 25 discusses the history of the Corps d'Afrique and its impact on later U.S. military operations.

3. For biographical material on the Roudanez brothers see *Our People, Our History* (Desdunes).

4. Chapter 5, "The Americanization of Black New Orleans 1850-1890", in *Creole New Orleans* (Hirsch) analyzes the Union Radical Association and the meeting with Lincoln.

5. For history and role of the Tribune see "Reconstruction Rebels: The New Orleans Tribune in Post-War Louisiana" (Connor). Poetry published in the Tribune is translated and studied for its political implications in "Creole Romantics on the Verge of a Nation" (Senter).

6. "The Negro in Louisiana" (Christian), chapters 27 and 28, detail this period.

7. This opinion is held by Marcus Christian in "The Negro in Louisiana", chapter 28. In the same chapter he also gives a comprehensive account of the Mechanics Hall Riot and the events that led up to it.

8. Besides Christian's account, the extent and effects of the massacre are interpreted in *Creole New Orleans* (Hirsch) chapter 5 and in "Race and Violence in Reconstruction New Orleans: The 1868 Riot" (Hennessey).

9. For more on the convention and its results see references of Christian and Hennessey mentioned above.

10. Lingering animosities after the riot are studied in "Race and Violence in Reconstruction New Orleans: The 1868 Riot" (Hennessey).

11. *The Chicory -Review* vol. 1, No. 2: spring 1989 published a transcript of the Citizens' Committee meetings and protest of attempts by whites to evict black lawyer Paul Bonseigneur and his family from their summer home in Mandeville, Louisiana in July 1893. *Creole New Orleans* (Hirsch) chapter 5 has more on the committee's role and activities.

12. For more on the political role of black women in this period see "The Negro in Louisiana" (Christian) chapter 29.

13. The altercation is recorded in *Creole New Orleans* (Hirsch) and "The Negro in Louisiana" (Christian).

Chapter 7:
The Creole Legacy Continues

1. For analysis of W.E.B. Dubois' views of the free people of color see the prologue to *Ambiguous Lives; Free Women of Color in Rural Georgia 1789-1879* (Alexander).

2. See the *Times-Picayune* August 16, 1993, section A page 7.

3. A comprehensive article on the Phipps case is "American Chronicles: Black or White" (Trillin). The case was also covered in the *Times-Picayune*, for example section 1 page 11 on Sept. 20,1982, and the front page on Sept. 26, 1982, May 19, 1983 and Dec. 9,1986.

4. See the *African Roots of Jazz* (Kaufman) p. 34-35. The transition of Creole music into jazz is clarified in "How the Creole Band Came to Be" (Gushee) and "Composers of Color of Nineteenth Century New Orleans: The History Behind the Music" (Sullivan).

5. The *Times-Picayune* ran a front page article January 17, 1994 tracing the ties of Martin Luther King to New Orleans.

6. Leah Chase, owner of Dooky Chase's restaurant in this Claiborne Avenue area, told the author how her business and life have been affected by the I-10 overpass. For decades her restaurant has served the Creole community of the city.

7. These observations were made by the author through association with Creoles in New Orleans.

8. See "California Creole", a two-part article in *Dixie* (Sunday supplement to the *Times-Picayune*) May 20, 1984 and
   May 28, 1984 which describes the Los Angeles Creole
   community and its ties to New Orleans.

Appendix

First and Last Names Common to Free People of Color

Because the free people of color in New Orleans spoke French and had French ancestors or took the names of French masters, most of their names were derived from that language and culture. During the Spanish period first names were often given a Spanish equivalent; e.g., Jean became known as Juan and Charlotte became Carlota.

Common first names among free women of color:

Adelaide/Adele, Agata, Aimée, Alexandrine, Angelique, Annette, Antoinette, Apolline, Athalie, Aurelia, Babet, Carmelite, Caroline, Catarina, Cecile/Cecilia, Celeste, Celestine, Charlotte, Clemence, Clementine, Constance, Delia, Delphine, Desiree, Dominique, Elizabeth, Emilie, Estelle, Eugenie, Eulalie, Euprosine, Fanchon, Felicie/Felicité, Francoise, Gabriela, Genevieve, Georgina, Elena/Helene, Heloise, Henriette, Ines, Isabelle, Isadora, Jeanne/Jeanette, Josephine, Julia, Juliette, Justine, Lisette, Louise(a), Magdalene(a), Manon, Manette/Nanette, Marceline, Marguerite, Marie(a), Marianne, Marthé, Martine, Mathilde, Modeste, Monique, Nathalie, Paulina, Pelagie, Perrine, Philomene, Poupon, Sanité, Serafine, Sophie, Suzanne, Rachel, Rosalie, Rosaline, Rose, Rosette, Teres/Thereze, Virgine, Victoire, Zelime/ Zulime.

Common first names among free men of color (note that many female and male names differ only by a letter or two in spelling):

Adolphe, Albert, Alcee, Alex, Alexandre, Alexis, Alphonse, Aime, André, Antoine, Armand, Auguste/ Augustin, Baptiste, Bartholomé/Barthelemy, Bazil, Benedicte, Bernard, Celestin, Charles, Charlot, Christophe, Clement, Edouard, Emile, Erasme, Etienne, Eugene, Ferdinand, Francois, Gabriel, Guillaume, Gustave, Henrí, Honoré, Hortense, Hypolite, Ignace, Isidore, Jacques, Jean, Joseph, Jules, Julien, Laurent, Leonide, Louis, Manuel, Marcel, Marcos, Martin, Mathieu, Michel, Narcisse, Nicolás, Noél, Olivier, Oscar, Paul/Pauline, Patrice, Pierre, Phillipe, Prosper, Rafael/Raphael, Raimond, René, Robert, Simon, Theodore, Theodule, Thomas/Tomas, Valentin(e), Victor, Vincent(e), Virgil, Xavier.

Common surnames among the free people of color in the French-Spanish colony pre-Louisiana Purchase (1803):

Almonester, Alpuente, Alva, Arnaud, Astier, Bacchus, Baure/ Borre/Porre, Boisseau, Brion, Brule, Burel, Campanel, Carriere, Cazelar, Cheval, Chouteau, Cienfuegos, Cofi/ Coffy, Darensbourg, Dauphin(e), Deco, Decoudreau, Delassize, Demezieres, Derneville, Despre, Dias, Dolliole, Dupart, Duplessis, Durand, Dutillet, Fazande, Forneret, Fouché(r), Galafate, Gaillard, Gallaud, Galvez, Genoveva, Garcin, Glapion, Hardy, Isnard/Hisnard, Heno, Hero, Hugon, Jeaneton, Juanico, Jung, Junon, Labastilier, Lacoste, Lalande, Lanuit,

LaPomeret, Labeau/Laveau, Lavolier, Leblanc, Lemelle, Lioutau, Livaudais, Luison, Macarty, Marcon, Maxent, Mallorquin/Mayorquin, Medor, Meilleur, Mercier, Metoyer, Mingo, Montplaisir, Montegut, Montreuil, Mounier, Navarro, Pascal, Peña, Peres, Piernas, Plessis, Pomet, Populus, Prudhomme, Quiñones, Raquet, Rami(s), Robin, Roché, Roque, Roquiny, Samba, Santiago, Sarasses, Scarasse, Sepion, Soulé, Soulie, Tiocou, Tio, Tisono, Totin, Toutant, Trudeau, Valdez, Vaugine, Venus, Vidal, Villemont, Villere, Vivant, Voisin, Viltz/Wiltz.

Additionally, there were these first names often used as surnames:

Alexis, André, Bernard, Fanchon, Marcos, Martin(a), Mathieu, Nicolas, Olivier, Raphael, Robert, Simon, Thomas, Xavier.

Common surnames among the free people of color in the years directly following the Louisiana Purchase (1803):

Many came from St. Domingue in the West Indies: Aleman, Allegre, Amothe/Lamothe, Bachemin, Bagneris, Baillio/Billie, Bajoliere, Baudin, Beaulieau, Beaumond(t), Beaurepaire, Bedeau, Bellaire, Bellevue, Beltremieux, Benoit, Bernoudy, Berque, Bertonneau, Bic/Bique, Boise, Bon/Bonne, Bondaille, Boni, Bonseigneur, Boutine, Boutte, Boyer, Cabaret, Cambray, Canelle, Caraby, Caresse, Cavalier, Cazenave, Chaigneau, Chretien, Colvis/Clovis, Cornier, Courcelle, Cournand, Couvertier, Croque/Crocker, Cupidon, Dalcour, Dapre-

129

mont, Daquin, Darcantel, Decourmant, Decuir, Dédé/Dedaio, Degre, Dejan, Delatte, Delille, Deruisseau, Desdunes, Deslisle, Deslonde, Destrehan, Dreux, Drouillard, Dubreuil, Dubuclet, Dumas, Dumois, Duplanchier, Dupuy, Dusuau, Duval, Duvernay, Esteves, Faucheaux, Faure/Favre, Ferrand, Ferrer, Florian, Fondall, Forstall, Fortier, Foy, Fressineau, Freyd, Frilot, Fuselier, Gandolfi, Gignac, Gillette, Glesseau/Gresso, Grammont, Grandmaison, Gravier, Greffen/Griffin, Guesnon, Guillmard, Guillory, Harang, Hart, Hazeur, Heguy, Henderson, Hobe/Jove, Houssart, Izard, Jalio, Jason, Jorda, Jordan, Joubert, Jourdain, Juncadella, Juin, Kernion, Kincaid, Lacled, LaCroix, Lafitte, Laforesterie, Lambert, Lamotte/Lamothe, Langlois, Lanna, Lanquille, Lanusse, Laroche, Laronde, Lasalle, Latapie, Larieux, Lavalle, Lavespere, Lavigne, LeClaire, Leclere, Leduc, Lefevre, Legoaster, Lemaitre, LeRoy, Llorens, Lorin, Loriot, Louyar, Lugar, Magliore, Malarcher, Mandeville, Mansion, Manumishon, Marchand, Marie/Mary, Marmiche, Martinez, Maurin, Mazant, Medard, Menard, Merrieult, Metzinger, Milon, Monsignac, Moreau, Morel, Moret, Morgan, Nelson, Nicaud, Noble, Norwood, Ortis(z), Ory, Othon, Ozee, Panis, Parent, Passebon, Pavegeau, Pedesclaux, Perrault, Peyroux, Picquery, Picot, Piron, Prevost, Prieto, Questi, Re, Rey, Reynaud, Rillieux, Rochon, Roich/Roig, Romain, Roup, Rousseau, Rousselle, Roy, Rouzan, Sabatier, Sainet, Sarasse, Savary, Seligny, Sejour, Senare, Ser/Serre, Sigur, Sindos, Soublet, St. Armand, St. Cyr, St. Denis, St. Julien, St. Martin, St. Ours, St. Victoire, Telemaco, Thezan, Thierry, Tinchant, Tonnelier, Toussaint, Tremé, Trevigne, Urquhart, Valcour, Valentin(e), Vallet, Valliere, Vernier, Villascusa, Vitrac, Volant, Warbourg, Williams, Zamora, Zeno(n), Zeringue.

Additionally, some first names were commonly used as surnames in this period:

Adolphe, Albert, Armand, Augustin(e), Baptiste, Barthelemy, Benjamin, Celestin(e), Christophe, Etienne, Francois, Guillaume, Henrí/Henry, Honoré, Hypolite, Isabel, Isidore, Iris, Jacques, Jean, Laurent, Manuel, Narcisse, Noel, Rose, Victor, Vincent.

From the 1820s through the Civil War there were free people of color from rural parishes moving into New Orleans. With them came additional French and German surnames. Many English surnames also began to appear as English owned slaves and descendants of American masters migrated to the city.

The above lists are not guaranteed complete. They are merely samples of names that appear repeatedly in records and writings of the period.

Appendix

Bibliography and Suggested Reading

Information for this book comes from the following sources. A few general works have been added as reference for further study.

The Colonial Period 1718-1803

Allain, Marthé. "Slave Policies in French Louisiana", *Louisiana History*, vol. 21 (Spring 1980) pp. 127-137.

Din, Gilbert C. "Cimarrones and the San Malo Band in Spanish Louisiana", *Louisiana History*, vol. 21 (Summer 1980) pp. 237-262.

Everett, Donald E. "Free Persons of Color in Colonial Louisiana", *Louisiana History*, vol. 7 (Winter 1966) pp. 21-50.

Fiehrer, Thomas. " Saint-Domingue/Haiti: Louisiana's Caribbean Connection", *Louisiana History*, vol. 30 (Fall 1989).

Hall, Gwendolyn Midlo. *Africans in Colonial Louisiana.* Louisiana State University Press, Baton Rouge 1992.

Hanger, Kimberly. "Household and Community Structure Among the Free Population of Spanish New Orleans 1778", *Louisiana History*, vol. 30 (Winter 1989) pp. 63-79.

Hanger, Kimberly. "Avenues to Freedom Open to New Orleans' Black Population, 1769-1779", *Louisiana History*, vol. 31 (Summer 1990) pp. 237-264.

Hanger, Kimberly. "Conflicting Loyalties: The French Revolution and Free People of Color in Spanish New Orleans", *Louisiana History*, vol. 34 (Winter 1993) pp 5-33.

Holmes, Jack D.L. "The Abortive Slave Revolt at Pointe Coupée, Louisiana, 1795", *Louisiana History*, vol. 11 (Fall 1970).

Johnson, Jerah. "New Orleans's Congo Square: An Urban Setting for Early Afro-American Culture Formation", *Louisiana History*, vol. 32 (Spring 1991) p. 117-157.

Mills, Gary B. *The Forgotten People: Cane River's Creoles of Color*. Louisiana State University Press, Baton Rouge, 1977.

Morazon, Ronald R. " 'Quadroon' Balls in the Spanish Period", *Louisiana History* vol. 14 (Summer 1973) pp. 310-315.

Usner, Daniel H., Jr. "From African Captivity to American Slavery: The Introduction of Black Laborers to Colonial Louisiana", *Louisiana History*, vol. 20 (Winter 1979) pp. 25-48.

Pre-Civil War Years 1803-1860

Alexander, Adele Logan. *Ambiguous Lives: Free Women of Color in Rural Georgia*, 1789-1879. The University of Arkansas Press, Fayetteville 1991.

Buckner, Alice Morris. *Towards the Gulf: A Romance of Louisiana*. 1887 (publisher not given).

Cable, George W. *Old Creole Days*. Scribner, New York 1879.

Cable, George W. *The Grandissimes*. Scribner, New York 1880.

Cable, George W. *Madame Delphine*. Scribner, New York 1881.

Christian, Marcus. *Negro Iron Workers of Louisiana 1718-1900*. Pelican Publishing Co., Gretna, La. 1972.

Christian, Marcus. *Negro Soldiers in the Battle of New Orleans*. 150th Anniversary Committee of Louisiana 1965.

De la Houssaye, Sidonie. *Les Quarteronnes de la Nouvelle Orléans*. Self-published in Bonnet Carre, La. 1894.

Detiege, Sr. Audrey Marie. *Henriette DeLille: Free Woman of Color*. Sisters of the Holy Family, New Orleans 1976.

Duchein, Mary Scott. *"Publication of Charles Gayarre's manuscript 'The Quadroons'"*, chapter 3 of "Research on Charles Etienne Arthur Gayarre", M.A. thesis, Louisiana State University, 1934

Gallaher, Mary Eugenius. *A History of St. Louis School of Holy Redeemer Parish*, New Orleans 1976.

Gehman, Mary. "The Louisiana Creole – Mexico Connection". *Louisiana Cultural Vistas,* winter 2001-2002, published by the Louisiana Endowment for the Humanities, New Orleans

Hunt, Alfred N. *Haiti's Influence on Antebellum America*. Louisiana State University Press, Baton Rouge 1988.

Ingraham, Joseph H. *The Quadroone; or St. Michael's Day*. Richard Bentley, London 1840.

Kendall, Lane Carter. "John McDonogh, Slave Owner", *Louisiana Historical Quarterly,* vol. 15 (October 1932) and vol. 16 (January 1933).

King, Grace. *Monsieur Mott*. A.C. Armstrong, New York 1888.

King, Grace. *New Orleans: The Place and the People*. Macmillan, New York 1895.

Loomis, Rosemary Fay. *Negro Soldiers – Free Men of Color in the Battle of New Orleans War of 1812*. Self-published in New Orleans 1991.

Raffalovich, George. *The Octoroon Case in Paris*. New York 1849.

Reid, Mayne. *The Quadroon*. Robert Dewitt, New York 1856.

Rice, Anne. *The Feast of All Saints*. Simon and Schuster, New York 1979.

Robin, C.C. *Voyage to Louisiana 1803-1805*. Abridged trans. Stuart O. Landry, Jr. Pelican Publishing Co., Gretna, La. 1966.

Rodriguez, Junius P. "Always 'En Garde': The Effects of Slave Insurrection Upon the Louisiana Mentality 1811-1815", *Louisiana History*, vol. 33 (Fall 1992) pp. 399-416.

Senter, Caroline. "Beware of Premature Autopsies: Hoodoo in New Orleans Literature", M.A. thesis, University of California, San Diego, 1991.

Schafer, Judith K. " 'Open and Notorious Concubinage': The Emancipation of Slave Mistresses by Will and the Supreme Court in Antebellum Louisiana", *Louisiana History*, vol. 28 (Spring 1987) pp. 165-182.

Schweninger, Loren. "A Negro Sojourner in Antebellum New Orleans", *Louisiana History*, vol. 20 (Summer 1979) pp. 305-314.

Sullivan, Lester. "Composers of Color of Nineteenth-Century New Orleans: The History Behind the Music", *Black Music Research Journal*, vol. 1: No. 1, 1988 pp. 51-81.

Tinker, Edward L. *Toucoutou* Dodd, Mead & Co., New York 1928.

Toledano, Rhoulac and Mary Louise Christovich. *New Orleans Architecture (series): Fauborg Tremé and the Bayou Road.* Vol. 6. Pelican Publishing Co., Gretna, La. 1980.

Webber, Everett and Olga. *Rampart Street.* E.P. Dutton & Co. New York 1948.

Whitten, David O. *Andrew Durnford: A Black Sugar Planter in Antebellum Louisiana.* Northwestern State University Press, Natchitoches, La. 1981.

Woodson, Carter G., ed. *Free Negro Owners of Slaves in the United States in 1830.* Negro Universities Press, Westport, Connecticut 1924.

Post-Civil War Years 1860-1920

Arthé, Agnes Anthony. "The Negro Creole Community in New Orleans, 1880-1920: An Oral History." PhD diss., University of California, Irvine, 1978.

Blassingame, John W. *Black New Orleans, 1860-1880*. The University of Chicago Press, 1973.

Connor, William P. "Reconstruction Rebels: The New Orleans Tribune in Post-War Louisiana", *Louisiana History*, vol. 21 (Spring 1980) pp. 159-181.

Gushee, Lawrence. "How the Creole Band Came to Be", *Black Music Research Journal*, vol. 8: No. 1, 1988 pp. 83-100.

Hennessey, Melinda Meek. "Race and Violence in Reconstruction New Orleans: The 1868 Riot", *Louisiana History*, vol. 20 (Winter 1979) pp.77-91.

Holditch, Kenneth W., ed. *In Old New Orleans*. University Press of Mississippi, Jackson 1983.

Rankin, David Connell. "The Forgotten People: Free People of Color in New Orleans 1850-1870." PhD diss., Johns Hopkins University, Maryland 1976.

Reinders, Robert C. *End of an Era: New Orleans 1850-1860*. Pelican Publishing Co., Gretna, La., 1964.

Reinders, Robert C. "The Free Negro in the New Orleans Economy, 1850-1860", *Louisiana History*, vol. 6 (Summer 1965) pp. 273-285.

Schweninger, Loren. "Antebellum Free Persons of Color in Postbellum Louisiana", *Louisiana History*, vol. 30 (Fall 1989) pp. 345-364.

Senter, Caroline. "Creole Romantics on the Verge of a Nation", unpublished manuscript, 1992.

Turner, Arlin. *George W. Cable: A Biography*. Louisiana State University Press, Baton Rouge 1966.

Modern Times to Present 1920-1994

Dominguez, Virginia. *White by Definition: Social Classification in Creole Louisiana*. Rutgers University Press, New Brunswick, N.J. 1987.

Faulkner, William. *Absalom! Absalom!* Random House, New York 1936.

Mullener, Elizabeth. "California Creole", *Dixie* (supplement to the *Times Picayune*), May 20,1984, pp. 9-16; May 28, 1984, pp. 8-18.

St. Julien, Aline. *Colored Creole: Color Conflict and Confusion in New Orleans*. Ahidiana Hobari Press, New Orleans 1977.

Trillin, Calvin. "American Chronicles: Black or White". T*he New Yorker* April 14, 1986, pp. 62-78.

Williams, Rebie Turnage. *Louisiana Love: Death Don't End it and Nothin' Don't Change it*. Wilfam, Inc., Chicago 1984.

General, Spanning all Time Periods

Borders, Florence, ed. *Chicory Review*. Bi-annual publication of the Chicory Society of Afro- Louisiana History and Culture, New Orleans.

Bryan, Violet Harrington. *The Myth of New Orleans in Literature: Dialogues of Race and Gender*. University of Tennessee Press, 1993.

Christian, Marcus. "The Negro in Louisiana" and "Black New Orleans, 1718-1938", unpublished manuscripts with Christian's papers at   the Library of the University of New Orleans, Special Collections.

Conrad, Glenn R. *A Dictionary of Louisiana Biography*. The Louisiana Historical Association, New Orleans 1988.

Desdunes, Rodolphe Lucien. *Nos Hommes et Notre Histoire*. Published privately in Montreal, Canada 1921. Translated as *Our People and Our History* by Sr. Dorothea Olga McCants and published by Louisiana State University Press, Baton Rouge 1973.

Hirsch, Arnold R. and Joseph Logsdon, eds. *Creole New Orleans: Race and Americanization*. Louisiana State University Press, Baton Rouge 1992.

Kaufman, Frederick and John P. Guckin. *The African Roots of Jazz*. Alfred Publishing Co., Inc. 1979.

Kein, Sybil. *Gombo People: New Orleans Creole Poetry*. Self-published in New Orleans 1981. Second expanded edition as *Gumbo People*, published by Margaret Media, Inc., New Orleans, 1999.

Kein, Sybil., ed. *Creole: The History and Legacy of Louisiana's Free People of Color.* Louisiana State University Press, Baton Rouge 2000.

Macdonald, Ronald R., John R. Kemp and Edward F. Haas, eds. *Louisiana's Black Heritage*. Louisiana State Museum, New Orleans, 1975.

Martin, Gilbert E. *Creoles: A Shattered Nation*. Self-published in New Orleans 1981

Perkins, A.E., ed. *Who's Who in Colored Louisiana.* Douglas Loan Co., Inc., Baton Rouge 1930.

Rousseve, Charles Barthelemy. *The Negro in Louisiana: Aspects of his History and his Literature*. The Xavier University Press, New Orleans 1937.

Saxon, Lyle and Robert Tallant, eds. *Gumbo Ya-Ya: Folk Tales of Louisiana*. Pelican Publishing Co., Gretna, La. 1987 (first edition 1945).

Wilson, Charles R. and William Farris, eds. *Encyclopedia of Southern Culture*. University of North Carolina Press, Chapel Hill 1989.

_____ "Together Apart: The Myth of Race" front page series in the *Times-Picayune*, appeared intermittently from May 9, 1993 to November 14, 1993.

_____ "The Vieux Carre Survey: A Pictorial Record and a Study of the Land and Buildings in the Vieux Carre." Prepared by Tulane University School of Architecture 1960-63, and housed in the Howard-Tilton Library at Tulane University.

Index

Dostie, Dr. A.P. 92

Dubois, W.E.B. 100, 125

Dubuclet, Antoine 3

Duke of Orléans 7

Dumas, Joseph 70

Dumas, Marguerite 70

Duncan Plaza 2

Dunn, Oscar J. 93

Dupuy, Edmund 89

Durnford, Andrew 76, 122, 137

Durnford, Thomas 76

E

Emancipation Proclamation 81, 86

Equal Rights League 89

Esplanade Avenue 37

Esteves, Arthur 72

F

Farragut, David 85

Fiehrer, Thomas 32

Fleming, Jean 69

Forneret, Joseph 49

Fouché, Louis Nelson 3, 72

Fouchér, Dutreuil 72

Fourth District Court of Appeals 103

France 5, 6, 10, 11, 17, 19, 25, 30, 46, 47, 48, 52, 62, 66, 70, 84, 86

Freedmen's Bureau 81, 90

Freetown 76

French Quarter 18, 33, 49, 53, 60, 107, 117

Frey Community 101

G

Gaillard, Elisabeth Aimeé 70

Gallaud, Luisa 40

Gallier Hall 51

Galvez, Bernardo de 41

Garrett, Mary 94

Gaspar, Marie 12

Gaudin, Juliette 74

Germany 19

Governor Allen 93

Grandjean 54

Guillory, Gregoire 103

Guimbilotte, Oscar 72

Gulf of Mexico 7, 56

Index

Index